OPTIONS TRADING

HOW TO TURN EVERY FRIDAY INTO PAYDAY USING
WEEKLY OPTIONS! GENERATE WEEKLY INCOME IN ALL
MARKETS AND SLEEP WORRY-FREE!

T. R. LAWRENCE

CONTENTS

INTRODUCTION

It was a beautiful Monday in South Florida. I was staring out the window of my office, teeing up the day, when my assistant came in and said my broker needs to talk with me right now, and she seemed upset. I said sure and took the call.

T.R.—a second of silence—Cisco has hit the floor, and this is a margin call. Can you bring a check for $1.4 million to cover it? I said "no." She said, "Okay, we will be liquidating your account."

I can personally guarantee you will never want to get a call like that in your life!

So, what happened?... The Dot.com Bubble.

Simple, I, like millions of others, confused brains with a bull market. From 1995 on, the market was on fire. Cisco, Intel, Microsoft, and Oracle were splitting 2 for 1 and sometimes 4 for 1, and it was insane. None of us had ever lived through anything like this, so we thought this was normal. Risk measures, sector balancing, and hedging were things others talked about. None of that applied to us!

When something catastrophic happens, you have two choices: Become a complete victim or find the gift or message. I admit, it was a little hard to think there was a gift here.

But there was—get educated!

Over the course of time, I hired a Goldman Sachs floor trader, took every course I could find, met and hung out with successful investors who kept making money in all markets, and learned what they knew. I did swing trading, and day trading; got into all kinds of technical analysis, and made better than decent money. However, it was like a full-time job, trading the open and then the close and doing other work in between.

Instead of being in front of my computer all day, I settled into selling monthly options and generating great cash. At that time, I sold covered calls on stocks I still owned, bought them for the trade, or sold puts for stocks that I wanted to own, just at lower prices.

Then, in 2010, Weekly Options were created, and life changed.

Why Are Weekly Options So Great!

I choose to trade weekly options for the following reasons:

- You can sell them four times a month! Repeat—4 times a month!
- The average premiums you collect are mostly *double* those sold for the monthly options—are you kidding?
- A 7-day time frame to manage risk and trends is easier.
- There are now hundreds of high-value stocks with weekly trading.

Who Is This Book For?

- Anyone who wants to generate an extra few hundred or thousand dollars a week to live without reducing the principle value of the account.

- Beginner investors who are curious about options and need a plan that gets them the most income with very manageable risk.
- Those will be small or large accounts.
- Experienced investors or traders that want to supersize their returns with less work.

What You Will Learn!

- All you need to know about Weekly Options to generate spendable cash.
- How to set up trades with complete sleep-at-night protection (no margin calls!)
- How to adjust trades in all markets.
- How to create a Trading Plan so trading is automatic and not emotional.
- How to make all the money you need and sleep well at night.

WHY I AM WRITING THIS BOOK

20+ years learning the tradecraft of trading and discovering what works for me.

Sometimes the best lessons and learning experiences happen after a catastrophe. The practice of selling options provides me with real peace of mind that I can generate cash to cover bills and my lifestyle without risking the farm. And I can do it from anywhere in the world that has an internet connection.

There is a freedom that comes with confidence—confidence that you own a thought process and techniques that will always take care of you and your loved ones. That is what this journey has given me.

And my hope is that you discover this as well.

Another beautiful aspect of this is visualizing the metaphor of a speed boat running circles around a giant aircraft carrier. *We* are the speedboats, the few retail traders left in the world that can move in and out of positions with lightning speed. The aircraft carriers are the large hedge funds with literally trillions of dollars under management that can't move that fast.

Finally, the last metaphor comes from that Goldman Sachs floor trader I hired to teach me. He said the market is like a giant Slurpee with a thick straw. You can suck as much money as you want out of it every day—and no one is going to look for it or care.

Give yourself permission to take it.

Therefore, I am giving you the same gift.

Trade on!

T.R. Lawrence.

1

UNDERSTANDING YOUR RELATIONSHIP WITH MONEY

> *Those who have knowledge of money make money their slave; but those who do not have knowledge of money becomes slave to it.*

— PRINCE EL FATI

Why are we talking about understanding your relationship with money in an options trading book? The reason for it is that we want to make money! We want to make a lot of it, and we want to keep it!

We want to make money for extra cash, security, or whatever we want. So, forget about what Mr. Market is doing for the next few minutes. That is only half of the equation. The other half is what is between your ears. It is your feelings, thoughts, and beliefs about money that matter.

Your relationship with money is not just about the numbers in your bank account or your financial situation; it is really a deep, complex, emotional connection that we all have with money, and it is shaped by our upbringing, our life experiences, and our personal values.

Understanding where we are in that relationship is the foundation for creating a healthier, more positive life in general because we all need money. However, as far as managing our finances in trading and setting up a trading plan, it is critical.

To begin recognizing your relationship with money, it is important to reflect on your experiences. Think about the messages you got growing up—were they positive or negative? Did you somehow learn to view money as a source of stress, conflict, or scarcity, or was it an abundance and an opportunity? Did you see parents or loved ones struggling with debt, experiencing financial distress, or experiencing financial success? Maybe both?

These are all beliefs that were shaped by the time we were five to seven years old. It goes a lot deeper, and there is a book forthcoming on this. However, the next couple of chapters will be a primer that, hopefully, will set the mindset. Your relationship with money is influenced by your personal values and your beliefs about the role of money in your life. For many, it just represents security and stability, while for others, it is a means to achieve their ultimate desires and make a positive impact. There is no right or wrong here. There is just what you feel about it. Recognizing this is the key to managing your intentions and creating a trading lifestyle.

UNDERSTANDING YOUR MONEY MINDSET

Once you become aware of the emotions and all the behaviors around money, you can adapt and learn to be more conscious and cultivate a more positive and empowering mindset, or if you already have a good mindset, discover how to supersize it and keep growing. How do you keep manifesting easily and effortlessly? We will discuss this in more depth, but I just want to start by having you become aware of any limiting beliefs or any negative self-talk that you may be processing for yourself. I mean, if you fundamentally believe that money is the source of all evil and is difficult to come by, this is going to lead to decisions that are based on fear and scarcity.

If you believe that money flows like a river and is abundant, that presents a distinct set of possibilities and outcomes. Also, once you define this positive mindset, it helps you make better decisions and easily prioritize your values and goals. If you have a clear understanding of what is important to you in life, you can make decisions that align with those values and goals.

If you come from a fear and scarcity mindset, it is like you are a TV set, and somebody else has the remote! You keep switching channels to do this and that based on fear. That is stressful. Overcoming those fears and getting to the root of core issues to understand and solve them helps set a great plan.

Developing a positive money mindset leads to overall well-being and quality of life. Yes, we want to have enough money to pay bills and live comfortably; however, really digging deep into this mindset so you see money flowing to you and how you keep it and attract more of it makes things a lot easier! We said this before: If you fundamentally believe that money is hard to come by or evil, well, it may not stick around for long! I know. I have personal experience with that and will share the story further on.

The bottom line is that how you feel about money and beliefs directly affects just about everything, even your physical health.

YOUR MONEY MINDSET IMPACTS YOUR QUALITY OF LIFE

Financial stress is a widespread problem for many people. If we are constantly worried about money, it leads to anxiety, depression, and other mental health issues. That is not a good place to be in. On the other hand, having a great relationship with money, even though you may desire more of it, creates an openness, acceptance, and vibration that you are worthy of all this abundance. Feeling in control of your finances because you have a healthy relationship boosts your confidence, reduces stress, improves your mood, and improves your sense of security. It may affect family relationships in positive or negative ways; financial issues are a common source of conflict in relationships.

If you and your partner have different values and beliefs around money, it can lead to some serious arguments where one person is living in scarcity and the other person is living in abundance. Suddenly, both sides are scared. Having a healthy relationship with money lets everyone breathe a sigh of relief that at least money and obligations are in good hands.

EXAMINING YOUR EXPERIENCES WITH MONEY

If you went back in time when you were five, seven, or eight years old, what was your life like? What memories are you having right now?

It is not just our upbringing that impacts the relationship. Any significant life events, such as job loss, illness, or divorce, can shape your mindset. I am laughing now, but I was not laughing at that time. If you remember my intro about how I began this journey by getting a huge margin call and being told to bring a monster check, or my account would be liquidated.

So yes, I could tell you categorically that I went into a scarcity mindset after that. I am not saying it was the best thing that ever happened to me, but within everything, there is a gift.

Why did it happen? How am I going to deal with it? At any given point in time, when you are faced with something like that, you can either be a victim or a survivor and step up to learn and not repeat it. Then establish ground zero for going forward.

If you grew up in poverty and experienced significant financial loss, those are deep-rooted beliefs attached to your soul level. We will discuss inherited beliefs further.

On the other hand, I recently met an amazing person who grew up with tremendous wealth—summer houses, a big yacht, the whole nine yards. One summer on holiday in the south of France when she was about 10, she was horrified that the other yacht owners had massive vessels compared to her family, and the kids looked down on her as not belonging there. She grew up with a scarcity mindset that took years to reconcile.

IDENTIFYING IMPORTANT MONEY BELIEFS

The first thing is to identify these beliefs, acknowledge them, and accept them. Many people get stuck with this —what do you mean, accept them? Once you acknowledge a belief, feeling, or situation, it "gets it out of you"— you are admitting it exists and are not in denial. And it is important to accept the situation you are in because, again, it is real.

That does not mean you are settling for it! Not in the least. It means this "is okay for now," but I am choosing to change this.

You may hate your job, yet you do not feel comfortable quitting because of finances. You are choosing to attract a better one, and in that instant of making that choice and opening up to wherever you believe information comes from, the healing process and new opportunities will start to flow in.

Once you identify each one, you go to work on the wording, and there are several resources. At the back of the book, there are programs and people that can help clear those blocks and go forward, but first, you have to be aware of them. That is step number one.

One thing to start doing now, no matter what, is to reframe any negative thoughts into something positive. I know that sounds all woo-woo, but I am a believer that your body hears every word you say. In fact, I think there is a book with that exact title. If you think about it, if you ask yourself, "How come I can't figure this out?" Your head's probably going to say, "Because you are not that smart!"

If you ask yourself the same question, "I wonder how to figure this out?" Well, that is a whole different feeling. You may even want to test that right now and see how you feel. When you say the magic words, "I wonder what is the best way to do this?" Then go for a walk or have a cup of coffee and stare out the window. You may be surprised at the information that starts to come back. When you change your words, you can clearly change your life.

RECOGNIZING YOUR MONEY'S STRENGTHS AND WEAKNESSES

Next is recognizing your strengths and weaknesses when it comes to money. There is no right or wrong here. Everyone is different.

One practice is to make a list of the things you are really good at and the things you are really bad at. The simplicity of life is to do what you are really good at and get some help with the areas you're not so good at.

It is fine if you do not feel you are good with money yet, because you can get a lot of help. If you are in need of a financial planner, then you could hire one. I thought I was good at trading and investing, but I confused brains with a bull market in the 90s. Looking back at those trades from my notes, I was way out of control, and no rules applied to me!

So, that was a weakness, and for me, I learned about it. The first thing I did when I got back on my feet was hire a coach. A fellow who was an experienced floor trader at Goldman Sachs. We restarted at ground zero and un-junked all my charts that had so many indicators that it was hard to see where the stock was trading! We just had support and resistance, or what some people call supply and demand. I learned all about when buyers turned into sellers and when sellers turned into buyers. Then I added just a few simple indicators for price action and volume, so I could clearly see the picture.

Also, relative to trading, I started as an intraday trader, and I was okay at it, but I was not great at it. It just seemed way too difficult and time-consuming for what I wanted to do with the rest of my life.

I really did not want to be tied to the market. Others, I know, do, and they love it. They trade the open; they trade the close; and they will do other things in the afternoon. It is a pure trading lifestyle, and they do really well. That did not work for me. I was looking for another avenue, and that is where I found the path to selling option premium. That has worked for me for a long time now.

ASSESSING YOUR PERSONALITY ABOUT MONEY—RISK ON OR RISK OFF?

Assessing your personality is critical. Are you somebody who is a risk-taker, or are you somebody who is risk-averse? Either one is fine, but if you are a risk-taker, which I was, it was safer and more profitable once I learned the rules of how to protect my positions! I did not do what I did before, which was totally blow up the accounts.

On the other hand, if you are someone who is very risk-averse, I really, truly believe that this trading style will make you smile because you are 100% in control of the level of risk. As you will learn in the meat and potatoes, how you set up your protection on these trades is the worry-free part of how you sleep at night.

At any given point, you may make what we call "a temporary investment into another person's account," another word for loss. Remember, your body hears every word! At the same time, by managing the program the way we do, we can often take that loss and roll it into the next week, generating enough instant cash to pay for the roll, so your new weekly cash-in covers the cash-out for the current week. If the stock rebounds, we will be profitable. If not, and we still decide to trade the stock, it is rinse and repeat.

There are lots of ways to mitigate risk. If you follow and set up your trading plan, you will never have a sleepless night, even if the market crashes as it did in March 2020 with COVID. I slept fine that night. All my long-term protection kicked in. It was fine. That would not have been the case 15 or 20 years ago.

OVERCOMING NEGATIVE THOUGHTS AND SELF-DOUBT

We all have doubts now and again. Any negative self-talk or limiting beliefs can totally sabotage your financial success. After all, we are humans! Everybody, no matter what, gets a twinge every once in a while.

If you have your plan in place, then you can work on visualizing that little self-doubt and picture it imprinted on a beach ball. When the ball comes, you just kick it down the road, and it is gone. You do not take the thought in and just push it away. Any statements that you have made in the past like I am terrible with money; I'll never be able to save enough for retirement; or I'll always be in debt, need to be batted away, and then set intentions of you overcoming those in seeing yourself.

Really, what we are talking about is being in the "now" to recognize those thoughts when they creep in. That is the way to overcome and neutralize them.

If you are setting up a trade or doing anything and all of a sudden fear enters, you have to recognize it. The more you recognize these limiting feelings, the more you bat them away, along with taking the right action that is totally congruent with your goals. You are not just closing your eyes and saying, "Go away," you have a plan of why it is going to work for you and execute it. Over time, they do not come up as much.

If you are cruising along and you do get a fearsome or negative thought that seems out of the ordinary, what I do is ask myself, "Where is this coming from? Did I hear something on the news? Did somebody say something to me that may have triggered an old response? Is there new information that changes my action plan?

FINDING THE ROOT CAUSE

Asking for guidance on where these feelings are coming from is critical so you can take action, clear them, and beat them all away. Again, I think there is a huge influence from friends, family, and culture, and going back to the earliest memories of money is kind of like watching your parents' behavior. If you had a family that argued about money and developed negative beliefs, then you probably saw it as negative. On the other hand, if your parents were financially savvy and encouraged you to explore, learn, and invest, you may have positive beliefs.

There is a great personal story here. There is a friend that I got to meet at a conference that we kept going to a few times a year. He is a well-established author, and he was telling the story one night of how he was teaching his young son about money.

They developed this plan called "Money Everywhere." When they would be out walking, the little one would find a penny, a nickel, a dime, or whatever. Over time, there was quite a large amount of money and even a few bills. What the young son was learning is that money is so abundant that people just leave it around!

WHAT A GREAT MINDSET!

I adopted it years ago and now have a section in my kitchen where I have all this change and many bills. I mean, it is hard to believe, really. The largest bill I found was a $20.00 bill, but I found that multiple times. I collected a lot of one-dollar bills and found a $5.00 bill about a month ago. I call that section of the kitchen "the money everywhere nook."

Even after all this time, it really helps reinforce the mindset. Occasionally I take some out, and I'll walk across the street to get a cup of coffee. Come on; it's a free cup of coffee; I found it, so it is abundant. Once you have that feeling, that feeling sticks.

EXPLORING INHERITED BELIEFS

We also inherit beliefs and habits. There is a great story about inherited beliefs. This little girl is watching her mom prepare a roast, and the mom cuts off the ends of the roast and puts it in the baking pan. The little one says, "Mommy, why did you cut the end off?" Mom says, "Well, that is the way my mom taught me."

So, the little one goes to Grandma and says, "Grandma, why did you teach Mom to cut off the end of the roast?" Grandma says, "Well, that is the way my mother taught me." Great-grandmother is still present, so the little one goes to great-grandma and says, "Why did you teach grandma to cut off the end of the roast?" Great Granny replies, "Well, when we got married, we only had one baking pan, and it was too small."

Think about that for a minute! You have three generations of people doing the same thing, and the root belief stems from the baking pan being too small!

If you think about that as far as sources of money beliefs, health beliefs, and expectations about life, these can have a huge impact on what is going on now.

Repeat the exercise, going back to when you were five or seven years old. Grab a sheet of paper and start writing down your beliefs about money and life in general. This time, look at them to see if you recognize any familiar ones from your parents, grandparents, or ancestors. This is very telling.

One inherited trait on the male side of our family was heart disease. My grandfather, father, and my dad's brothers all had heart issues. When my older brother had a triple bypass, his cardiologist asked if he had any brothers and recommended that I get checked out because I had that family trait.

At that time, I was working with a physician more from the perspective of being healthy and staying that way versus getting sick and then calling a doctor! Anyway, my doctor said that I was certainly going to die of something; however, it probably was not going to be heart disease because I never went to war, had severe PSTD, did not smoke, did not drink too much, and always had a healthy diet. And, exercise was a way of life.

As you start to go down that rabbit hole, I believe you will gain clarity. Next, start putting together your financial goals. From this perspective, you will be better aligned with your new money habits.

Finally, once you get through those goals and relate them to the trading plan we will put together, you will have a solid foundation.

You can start crafting a simple but articulate trading plan. My plan serves as an example. I have a percentage of risk on each trade, and I *do not* deviate. My goal is to make 1% a week of deployed capital. So, that is an annualized return of 52% a year. It may seem outrageous when the S&P is doing 10 or 12%, but 1/2% a week is 26%. When you chunk out the math and take a look at what the option premiums are versus what the risk is, you will clearly see that this is more than doable. You will be able to do this. There are ups and downs, but across the board, you will be able to achieve that if you keep learning and have a solid plan.

DEEPER INTO CHILDHOOD EXPERIENCES

I want to go back to the impact of childhood experiences to dig a little deeper. I grew up in a household where we had what we needed. I came from a blue-collar family. Mom and Dad worked. We always had clothes. We always had food. We had a nice house. However, they worked hard for the money.

However, there was duality and conflict. On one side, my mom would put me to bed at night and say, "Someday, I'm going to invent something or do something and become a millionaire. Also, if I could read, I could do anything." So, guess what happened to me? I mean, I am an incessant reader, even today. And I became financially secure relatively early in my life. (We will talk about keeping it later!)

Then on the other side was my dad. I do not remember how young I was one day when I innocently asked him how much money he made. He got angry and defensive and said, "We do not talk about those things." That was a total blindside.

On one side of it, there is this complete abundance-flow mindset from my mom, and on the other side, there is this giant negativity. Then it got worse.

I was confused and felt really stuck. Then I got severe asthma, and since mom was a nurse, her mantra became, "Don't do too much." I know she loved me and was being protective; however, one side was full throttle, and the other was secret, so don't do too much!

As I began my career, the swings were huge, managing to attract all this amazing abundance and then seeing it slip away as the "don't do too much belief" came roaring in. The infamous margin call was the classic example of giving it back, resulting from this belief. I did not have any beliefs that *allowed* me to keep any of it!

This happened to me a number of times, and I felt like I was a yo-yo and someone else was in complete control. It was not until I recognized the mindset and pattern and said, "Okay, I get it; I am choosing a different path here."

Acknowledging and changing that mindset was and continues to be one of the best things I have ever done. It was hard work to dig all that up.

Now it is your turn!

What is *your current money mindset?*

So, after all this, what is your current money mindset?

When you start thinking about money, do you feel excited? Do you feel anxious and different—something else? That question is a powerful starting point. Just about everybody has an emotional response, whether they realize it or not. For some, money triggers, as I said, feelings of stress, anxiety, and worry. Others feel excitement, joy, and a sense of power when they think about money. Some people are completely indifferent or neutral, and they just view it as a practical necessity rather than an emotional topic. It is important to say that there is no right or wrong here. It is just what you feel, and if that feeling is serving you, great. If it isn't, then you basically change it.

Does your attitude toward money change depending on the context? Do you feel one way about money when you think about your own finances versus those of someone else? How do your feelings about money affect your behavior? Do you avoid thinking about it because it stresses you out, and you just turn a blind eye?

I had a friend years ago who was a very successful executive. Her mom and dad had lost a lot of money in a business, and she had a complete block about dealing with money, and it was amazing. I walked into her office, and there was a guy, literally named Rocco, there who was repossessing her car. I asked myself how this could possibly be happening because I knew how much money she was making and that she drove a Miata, not a Ferrari. She was so blocked about money that it was hard for her to make a simple car payment.

Do you obsess over it? Do you spend it impulsively, or do you save every penny? These are important things to journal about. Once you can get through those, changing or improving your mindset is the next step. List any of the limiting beliefs or negative self-talk that you may have about money from the previous exercises. Tuck them away in a journal.

You will have a process to work through when these beliefs come in. You can see them printed on a beach ball and then bat them away. When these beliefs come in, you could work harder at reframing them from any of the negative talks. Like, if it is, "I'll never be wealthy, or I am terrible with money," that could easily be reframed with something like, "Isn't it great that I am learning how to be good with money? Isn't it great that I am finally learning how to do this? I wonder how to do this," and see that beach ball and go, then take a walk around the block and see what comes back.

YOUR JOURNEY BEGINS TODAY

The journey on this really begins today, and developing a more positive and empowering money mindset will help you approach money challenges with confidence and resilience and overcome just about anything in your life. This is about more than money. Once you are in that positivity, all of a sudden, you have a different vibration. People look at you differently. You walk into the store, and someone says, "How are you?" Instead of saying, "Hanging in there." How did those words feel versus "I am great?" This mindset now gives you abundance and positivity because of your willingness to learn and grow.

You can view setbacks as opportunities. As I said, going back to the margin call, I really wish that did not happen, but it was a defining factor that changed my life for the better. All those years of not understanding that process.

Once your greatest fear has been realized and you have overcome it, then you really walk differently as a human being. Success now is not new to you because you know what it feels like, looks like, and tastes like. You also know exactly what you do not want and are able to change the channel on those thoughts and actions to bat them away.

DEVELOPING A GROWTH MONEY MINDSET

A growth mindset is the end goal. Things do not go in a straight line, as we said. Every once in a while, we'll make a temporary investment into someone else's account and learn to roll and manage trades. How to rinse and repeat and create your personal ATM, drawing out as much cash as you want.

The basis of the growth mindset revolves around reframing the negative thoughts of developing a learning process and willingness to learn to the point where you are always growing, and nothing is static. I learn new things all the time looking at the markets, looking at companies, and looking at charts.

There will be a section later in the book about how to supersize trades. Our KaChing method works and is solid and repeatable, but there are ways to supersize it if market conditions are favorable. I was not doing that a few years ago, but now I am, and the extra cash flow is great. We are always growing.

GRATITUDE IS THE KEY

One of the greatest positive elements of this process is the practice of gratitude. When I take the time to be grateful and write down what I am grateful for that day, it is comforting, and there is an unmistakable feeling of warmth.

It could be anything: Finding a parking space on a busy street just when you need it, a sudden windfall, or an answer to something you were working on. As you give thanks and recognize that synchronicity, it is amazing, and more just keep coming.

I keep a gratitude journal and take a few minutes to write those things down, but more importantly, what do they feel like? As the journal pages fill up, one thing becomes very clear: There is no shortage of miracles available, and it makes me feel connected and great.

DEALING WITH NON-SUPPORTIVE PEOPLE

This is not anyone's favorite thing to deal with. However, moving forward with your mindset means working to surround yourself with people who are positive and supportive. Sometimes that can be challenging, especially if some of those people are family members. They may not see eye-to-eye with what you are attempting to do. If there are beliefs that come up like, "Well, you can't do that, or that is not for you, or you *do not* know anything about that," then you must reframe all those. No one knows about anything until they learn about it, right?

Some of this is done for protection because they do not want to see you hurt. Other times, they see you taking action and becoming successful, and it points out their lack of action or awareness and makes them feel bad.

As I was coming up through the entrepreneurial ranks, I worked in Silicon Valley for a number of years, and I got to a point where I started to have nicer cars than some of my friends, and this and that. It was hard to process because they started treating me differently. A mentor helped me with the process and to accept that some would stay friends and others would go, and it was okay. I was taking action and was the one working weekends and taking courses, and they weren't. His comment to me was, "You do now what others will not, so later you do what they cannot."

It is hard to get rid of a toxic family member; however, you can set boundaries for what you are available for. You always stay in love, no matter what, but you can make a choice: "Hey, I love you. However, I choose not to be around you right now if (whatever persists)."

In my opinion, it is okay to do that. There may be times when someone tells you that you are being selfish—that is tough—what I learned over the years was that it was a compliment (assuming you are not me, me, and only me and are not helping where you are able). And the reason is that I was making my own choices for how to live my life and was not going to live the life that someone wanted for me because they had remorse or it was some kind of family tradition.

CREATE A VISION BOARD

Another exercise that I like is creating a vision board. Something bold that keeps my plan and intentions front and center daily.

I am visual, but even if you are not, you could have a board where you write down all your goals. Financial, both short-term and long-term. My current version has rotating 90-day goals to keep moving, all tied into the master goal, where I see the whole picture.

Include great pictures of some things that you want to bring into your life. It could be your perfect mate. It could be a living situation. When you define your goal, see it, and keep seeing it over and over, it becomes real because your subconscious mind doesn't know the difference between thinking about something and seeing something that is real. So, if you see it, then it becomes very real. Be precise about what you want to achieve financially. Do you want to pay off all your debt? Do you want to save for a down payment on a home? Do you want to start investing? Be specific.

Then get all your materials. You get a big poster board, a bunch of magic markers, and a cork board, and have some fun on this. You could do it digitally as well. I do not like to do that. I am a tactile person. I like to see the board in front of me until it becomes real. I look at it every day just as an affirmation that everything is there, and it really makes a big difference.

So, with all that said, once you understand your mindset, changing it is a process that could take time, but it starts with knowing what your beliefs are and really knowing them. And for that, you have a blueprint.

Congratulations! You have gone deep into this, and it can be hard work dredging up old thoughts and beliefs. I guarantee you that the end result of this is going to be a really positive mindset where you wake up in the morning relaxed and with a clear plan.

2

STOCK MARKET PSYCHOLOGY

The stock market doesn't only teach how to make money but it also teaches lot about life, patience, persistence and wisdom.

— RAJ MISHRA

Stock market psychology is all about the way our thoughts and feelings impact how we behave in the stock market. It's a mix of our biases, emotions, and other psychological factors that shape our decisions about whether to buy, sell, or hold on to stocks. These psychological factors can influence both individual investors and wider market trends, which can lead to crazy situations like market bubbles, panics, and crashes.

Understanding stock market psychology is key for traders and investors who want to make good decisions, control risk, and succeed over the long term.

When it comes to shaping stock market psychology, the big players known as "institutional market makers" hold a lot of sway. These heavyweights are usually banks, investment firms, and hedge funds that trade large amounts of securities. They can make a real impact on the market because their massive investments can move mountains, causing stock prices and market trends to shift.

Institutional market makers have a few different ways they can shape market psychology. For instance, if they buy up a bunch of a certain stock, it can signal to other investors that the stock is ripe for picking or has potential for growth. This can create a buying frenzy that pushes the stock price up and sets a positive tone in the market.

On the flip side, if an institutional investor sells off a lot of a certain stock, it can signal to other investors that the stock is overvalued or not likely to grow much more. This can create a selling frenzy that drags the stock price down and sets a negative tone in the market.

THE ANALYST CARTEL

There is a term often used to describe the big institutions: The Analyst Cartel. Nothing is done without purpose. We talk about "the trend being our friend" and liken the stock market to a huge wave—if you are flowing with the wave, you are fine; if you are swimming against it, you better get off, or you will get crushed.

My coach showed me how to look at a chart without a lot of junked-up indicators—basically, just price action and volume—so that you could clearly see the tops and the bottoms. When there is a reversal from the top, buyers turn into sellers, and from the bottom, sellers turn into buyers.

Often, a stock can run up for a lot of reasons, and everyone is making money. Then suddenly, there is a downgrade or talking ahead opinion that does not immediately point to more growth. Then some selling occurs, then a little more, and all of a sudden, there is a large volume sell-off, and people are selling like crazy to avoid losses.

What really happened? (This does not include a catastrophic event like sudden financial news where the Chief Financial Officer resigned to "spend more time with the family" or a drug company failing FDA approval.)

The Cartel made a lot of money in the run-up. So they may create a selling atmosphere where retail traders who listen to the TV talking heads get scared and preserve any profits—they sell.

The stock comes back down, and the Cartel is very happy. Suddenly there is an upgrade, and the stock starts to move up again. What happened is that the Cartel took the place of the sellers and bought much, much lower, so they can ride it back up again!

Look at these charts with gaps in the opposite direction.

Amateur Gap

You can see the stock is moving up; then suddenly, there are *large* gaps up and up with heavy volume. These are *not* institutional purchases! This is people listening to a talking head before going to work, saying this stock is going to rip, and FOMO (fear of missing out) roars in. Never fall for this; the street calls it "dumb money." On the mid to far left of the chart, there are two examples of Pro Gaps – suddenly moving in the opposite direction. Buying at the top is always risky!

Professional Gap

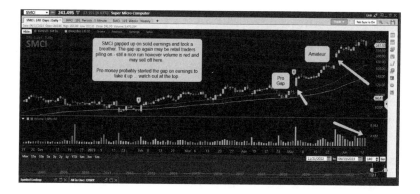

Professional Gaps are identified by sudden, larger moves in the opposite direction with volume. In the instance above, you can see the possible Pro Gap from earnings. The market makers are taking it up. Later, probably with an analyst recommendation, there are retail traders jumping in – classic Amateur Gap. Watch out at the top!

PRICE LINE STORY—A CLASSIC EXAMPLE OF MANIPULATION

A classic that happened to me several years ago was Price Line. Price Line can cover a lot of ground, and $100 swings were not unusual. The chart looked compelling, and the earnings whisper was that earnings were going to be a blowout. I bought what they call a strangle pre-earnings—an at-the-money call and a put at the same strike price with the same expiration date—to hedge. One side would make money, and the other would lose money; the drill was to exit the losing position quickly and get the most out of the winner.

Earnings after the close were a pure blowout. After hours, the stock was up $65. I was salivating, waiting for the market to open.

Before the open—Goldman Sachs issues a downgrade! The US numbers were amazing; however, they did not like the softness of guidance in Europe. Really? At the open Price Line sold off with large volume and sunk more than $100! I did okay with the hedge. However, any directional traders on the long side would have been crushed.

Sixty days later, with Price Line still down over $100, Goldman issued an upgrade on the softness in Europe, saying it was looking better. Right! And the stock moved right back up.

All in all, institutional market makers are a big deal when it comes to shaping stock market psychology. Their actions and words can really impact other investors and set the tone for the market's behavior.

FEAR AND GREED

Fear and greed are two emotions that have a significant impact on the stock market. Fear can cause investors to panic and sell their stocks, while greed can lead to irrational buying behavior and excessive enthusiasm —Amateur Gaps. These emotions can cause volatility in the market and have unintended consequences for investors.

To manage fear and greed, investors can start by setting clear investment goals and developing a well-thought-out trading plan. This can help investors avoid making impulsive decisions based on emotional responses to market fluctuations. With a solid plan, the emotion is removed, and you just execute.

It is also important for investors to monitor their emotions and be aware of how they are feeling when making trades. The "felt sense" helps investors identify when they are experiencing fear or greed and take steps to manage these emotions before making a decision.

For example, if your trading plan dictates that no more than 2% of the portfolio value be allocated to any single trade, and you *really* want to load up on something that takes the percentage to 10%, you may feel a little stressed (I hope so!). At all times, be in the present so you do not miss warnings like this. Of course, if you have a larger portfolio and feel safe with higher percentages, then adjust. Do not make a fearful or greedy decision.

For the way we trade using the KaChing method with vertical spreads, you could hedge risk by tightening the spread difference, so instead of a 5-point spread, you can do a 3-point or even a 2-point spread or take less contracts.

Managing fear and greed is essential for investors to succeed in the stock market. By setting clear goals, monitoring emotions, using risk management tools, and seeking support when needed, investors can make informed decisions and avoid being driven solely by emotional responses to market fluctuations.

Herd Mentality

Herd behavior in the stock market can be a double-edged sword. On the one hand, following the crowd can provide a sense of safety and reassurance that others are making the same investment decisions. However, it can also lead to irrational and uninformed decision-making, which can have disastrous consequences, like falling for Amateur Gaps.

One of the main problems with herd behavior is that it can create market bubbles. This happens when investors become overly optimistic about a particular asset, driving its price up beyond its fundamental value. As more and more investors pile into the asset, the price becomes increasingly detached from its true value, creating a bubble. Eventually, the bubble bursts, and the asset price crashes, leaving investors who bought in too late with significant losses. One data point for me back in the day was when cab driver's gave stock tips!

Herd behavior can also contribute to market crashes. When investors begin to panic, they may rush to sell their investments, causing a chain reaction that can lead to a sudden and steep drop in asset prices. This can create a negative feedback loop, with falling prices leading to more selling and further price declines.

To manage the risks associated with herd behavior, it's important for investors to do their own research and not rely solely on the opinions of others. At all times, you want to discover what the professionals are doing and follow them.

Investors Daily (or other tools)

I use Investors Daily to look at stocks, trends, and sectors. One tool I always look at is the accumulation/distribution rating. I do this for indices like the S&P, DOW, and NASDAQ, as well as for stocks. When you see a sudden 2-grade increase or decrease, no matter where the market is, you must take notice. In a bearish market, the A/C index will begin to move up before you see any increase. You just take note that the pro-market makers are feeling pretty good.

It's the same in reverse. The trend is our friend!

Herd behavior is a powerful force in the stock market and can lead to irrational and uninformed decision-making. By doing your own research, diversifying your trades into different sectors, and above all, following your trading plan, you will always be on the right wave!

BELIEF REINFORCEMENT BIAS

Belief reinforcement, or confirmation bias, is a common psychological phenomenon that can have a significant impact on how investors make decisions in the stock market. This bias refers to the tendency of people to seek out information that supports their pre-existing beliefs while ignoring evidence that contradicts them.

Confirmation bias can lead investors to make decisions that are not based on objective information and may lead to incorrect conclusions about the market. For example, if an investor is bullish on a particular stock, they may only seek out information that supports their view while ignoring information that suggests the stock may be overvalued or have limited growth potential.

We have all suffered this at one time or another. Years ago, I was assigned shares when a KaChing trade went south, and the stock was given to me. That is never an issue because the very next day, I could have sold the stock, cashed in the long protective put, kept all the premium, and just been responsible for the difference—in that case, it was $2.50 on 1,000 shares or $2,500. I could have immediately gotten back into the trade and sold my way back to profit, assuming there was still a reason to be in that stock.

Instead, I became an "investor." Oh yeah—I wanted to own the stock anyway; it will move back up, and this is long-term." Was any of that in my first Trading Plan–NO! Long story short, I sold covered calls on a weekly basis and made the $2500 back. In the meantime, the stock had slipped further down. And in a few months, it was back up and just bouncing around.

I finally figured it out—this was dead money. Yes, it will go up, and the long-term prospects are solid (and it is doing great at the time this book is being written). However, when I sold and took the cash to deploy to a current set of trades, I made a lot more money!

One way to manage confirmation bias is to seek out diverse sources of information and perspectives, like looking at the Accumulation/Distribution index and looking at price action and volume daily—there is no story here for the time being.

This can help investors challenge their own assumptions and consider alternative viewpoints that may contradict their beliefs. Additionally, investors can benefit from regularly reviewing their Trading Plan investment strategies and challenging their own assumptions.

It is important to really understand our personal biases and tendencies. Do you really like to be right all the time? When new information is presented, do you hang on to your beliefs or openly look at the new "evidence" and make an informed decision?

Or conversely, if you lack confidence in trading, is it your fundamental belief that you will get it wrong? Both are very dangerous. And both can be overcome with unemotional tools and a great trading plan where your sleep-at-night risk is in place.

PAINFUL LOSS SYNDROME

Loss aversion is a common bias that can have a significant impact on investment decisions. It is the tendency of investors to feel the pain of losses more acutely than the pleasure of gains. This can lead them to hold onto losing positions for too long, hoping that the market will turn around and they can recoup their losses.

The best way to manage loss aversion is to establish a clear investment strategy, such as a Trading Plan, and stick to it. We have reconciled that sometimes we will make a temporary investment in someone else's account. It is OK! Give yourself permission to be OK as long as you are following your plan and adjusting it if needed.

ARE YOU MORE AFRAID OF LOSING THAN WINNING?

This may sound odd; however, think about it. In a world where "winning is everything" and no one remembers the runner-up in the Super Bowl, being a *loser* is toxic. It is scary and leads to a scarcity mindset.

I first learned this as an up-and-coming tennis player. My coach told me that the person I was playing with was more scared of losing than winning. At the time, I did not really understand. The coach said if I put on the heat on the return of serve and got him worried, he would go into fear mode and start being more conservative.

So, I did. I just banged that first serve back, missing more than making; however, a few went in for winners, and suddenly, I was getting second serves that looked like beach balls, so I cranked up the heat even more!

In my professional life as part of a venture capital fund, I saw it with entrepreneurs. Getting their companies off the ground takes a lot of time, and most of the time, they never have any money. That leads to a mindset of preserving cash as the holy grail. In their pre-investment state, this was certainly true. However, after a healthy first-round investment when there is all the cash to fund expansion, often we could not get the entrepreneurs to spend any of it!

WHAT'S THE SOLUTION?

Have a plan and roadmap; surround yourself with a team, mentors, and people you follow; and above all, have the mindset that "I am always in the right place at the right time, and things mostly work out fine." The word "mostly" gives some latitude.

There are weeks when I am rolling over trades into the next week as the market gyrates. It does not affect me now; my plan is in place, and some red ink means nothing compared to the profits already earned and in the future. In fact, recently, I was in the third week of rolling and looked at my trade log for each trade. Yes, red, red, red for 3 weeks. However, volatility was very high, meaning the option premiums I was selling each week to roll were fat!

In week 4, rolling an at-the-money put brought in enough premium to wipe out the previous 3 weeks and give me a great profit. I felt extreme gratitude each week, even though the first three did not pan out. When I banked that premium at the end of week 4, it was sweet —I cracked open a cold one! Trust the plan.

OVERCONFIDENCE

Overconfidence is a common phenomenon that affects investors in the stock market. This tendency is characterized by investors who believe that they can beat the market and consistently outperform other investors. This behavior is often driven by the belief that they possess unique insights or abilities that allow them to achieve superior returns.

In other words, confusing brains with a bull market and having so much success that there is a belief that the rules do not apply to you.

The worst thing that happens is taking some of these risks and having them go your way! All that says is more, and more, and more because you are invincible. Then there is a reckoning, and often the losses are catastrophic.

This applies to life as well. I was a police officer for a while (yes, I have been a lot of things), and we saw it all the time, especially drinking and driving. Getting back safely is always great; however, gaining the belief that you are a great driver under the influence leads to disaster in most cases.

Back to trading: "Getting paid to break the rules" is not a winning course of action.

Overconfidence leads investors to take excessive risks. An overconfident investor may believe that they can accurately predict the market or that they possess inside information that other investors do not. This can lead them to make large, concentrated bets on individual stocks, which can result in significant losses if those stocks do not perform as expected.

To manage overconfidence, investors need to remain humble and recognize their limitations. This means acknowledging that there is a degree of uncertainty in the stock market and that even the most experienced investors can make mistakes.

And, as we are ramming home, a solid Trading Plan eliminates the emotions of trading.

FIRST IMPRESSION BIAS

First Impression bias or Anchoring bias is a cognitive bias that can affect the decision-making process of investors. It occurs when investors rely too heavily on the first piece of information they receive when deciding, even when new and contradictory information becomes available.

This tendency to "anchor" on the initial piece of information can lead to flawed decision-making as it limits an investor's ability to consider new information or perspectives. Investors may become overly attached to their initial beliefs and fail to adjust their positions accordingly.

For example, an investor who buys a stock based on a positive news report may become anchored on the initial information and fail to sell the stock even if subsequent news indicates that the company is experiencing financial difficulties. This can result in significant losses if the investor continues to hold onto the stock despite mounting evidence to the contrary.

First Impression Bias can be difficult to overcome at first. A strategy is to regularly reassess one's decisions and adjust positions as necessary based on new information. By remaining open to new perspectives and being willing to change their minds, investors can avoid becoming anchored to a single viewpoint and make more informed decisions.

DECISION AVOIDANCE SYNDROME

Decision avoidance, also called "Regret Aversion," is a common phenomenon that can have a significant impact on investor behavior. Investors who suffer from regret aversion tend to avoid making decisions that could lead to regret, even when those decisions may be rational and in their best interest. This can lead to missed opportunities, lower returns, and a failure to diversify their portfolios.

The fear of regret is a powerful emotion that can cause investors to focus on avoiding losses rather than maximizing gains. This can result in a reluctance to take risks and a tendency to stick with familiar investments, even when they may not be the best choice. For example, an investor who has suffered losses in a particular stock may be hesitant to sell it, even if there is evidence that the stock is likely to continue declining.

One of the ways that regret aversion can be managed is by setting clear investment goals and sticking to a well-defined Trading Plan. This helps investors avoid making emotional decisions based on short-term market fluctuations or the fear of missing out on potential gains. A disciplined approach to investing can also help reduce the impact of regret aversion by providing a clear framework for decision-making and minimizing the impact of emotional biases.

Another way to manage regret aversion is to practice mindfulness and self-awareness. By acknowledging and understanding the impact of emotions on investment decisions, investors can develop strategies to overcome the fear of regret and make more rational and objective decisions. This can involve techniques such as journaling, meditation, or seeking the advice of a financial advisor who can provide an objective perspective on investment decisions.

There are literally millions of potential stock trading opportunities. If you miss one, another one comes along, like cars passing you on the street. Be patient!

COGNITIVE DISSONANCE

Cognitive dissonance is a common phenomenon experienced by investors and can significantly affect their decision-making. This is the discomfort felt when their beliefs and actions are in conflict. Investors often hold certain beliefs or biases about the market or specific investments, and when their actions contradict those beliefs, cognitive dissonance can occur. This can lead to irrational decision-making, where investors may try to justify their actions to themselves and others, even if they do not align with their beliefs.

For example, an investor may believe that investing in a particular company is a sound decision. However, if the company releases poor financial results, the investor may be faced with cognitive dissonance as their belief in the company's potential conflicts with the new information. In this scenario, the investor may try to justify their decision to hold onto the investment despite the new information suggesting that it may not be the best choice.

To overcome cognitive dissonance, investors need to be open to challenging their beliefs and biases. This requires a willingness to seek out new information, even if it contradicts their existing beliefs. One way to do this is by actively seeking out opposing viewpoints or conducting research that challenges their existing beliefs. By doing so, investors can gain a more comprehensive understanding of the market and make more informed decisions.

At the end of the day, it is simple once you get your head out of the way. It goes back to why this stock is trading right now. We trade what we *see*, not what we *believe*.

Investors can work to manage their emotions when making investment decisions. Cognitive dissonance is often driven by emotions, and by remaining objective and rational, investors can reduce the impact of these emotions on their decision-making.

Cognitive dissonance can have a significant impact on investor decision-making, leading to irrational choices and self-justification. However, by challenging their beliefs, seeking new information, seeking advice, managing emotions, and remaining objective, investors can overcome cognitive dissonance and make more informed decisions.

MARKET SENTIMENT

Market sentiment refers to the collective emotions and attitudes of investors toward the stock market. It can be influenced by a variety of factors, including economic news, political events, and corporate earnings reports. Understanding market sentiment is essential for investors to make informed decisions about buying and selling stocks.

Market sentiment can be classified as bullish or bearish. A bullish sentiment indicates that investors are optimistic about the market's future and that stock prices are likely to rise. Conversely, a bearish sentiment indicates that investors are pessimistic and stock prices are likely to fall. One way to use market sentiment to your advantage is by keeping an eye on market indicators such as the volatility index (VIX) and the put-call ratio. The VIX is a measure of the market's volatility and can be used to gauge investors' fear or uncertainty. A high VIX indicates that investors are anxious and very fearful, and the market may be due for a correction. A lower VIX reading signals market complacency and a low level of fear. Contrarian traders often see a low VIX as a bearish sign. If the market is overbought, any market event could spike sales.

The put-call ratio measures the ratio of put options (options to sell) to call options (options to buy). A high put-call ratio indicates that investors are bearish, while a low put-call ratio indicates bullish sentiment.

Overcoming cognitive biases like confirmation bias and overconfidence can also help investors use market sentiment to their advantage. By being aware of their biases and actively seeking out information that contradicts their beliefs, investors can make more informed decisions and avoid falling prey to the herd mentality.

IS MARKET SENTIMENT THE SAME AS HERD MENTALITY?

While following market sentiment can sometimes lead to herd mentality, it is possible to use market sentiment to your advantage without falling into this trap. One way to do this is to use market sentiment as a contrarian indicator. For example, if the market sentiment is overwhelmingly positive, it may be a signal that the market is overheating and is due for a correction. In this case, a contrarian investor might look for opportunities to short the market or invest in undervalued assets that are out of favor with the crowd.

Here is a great quote from Warren Buffett: "Buy when there's blood in the streets, even if the blood is your own."

Another way to use market sentiment to your advantage is to analyze it in conjunction with other factors, such as economic indicators, industry trends, and company-specific news. By taking a holistic approach to market analysis, you can gain a more nuanced understanding of the market and make more informed investment decisions.

As we discussed previously, my favorite market sentiment indicator is the Accumulation / Distribution index. This is the pure money flow of what the institutions are doing.

Understanding market sentiment is crucial for investors looking to make informed decisions about buying and selling stocks. By keeping an eye on market indicators, conducting sentiment analysis, and overcoming cognitive biases, investors can use market sentiment to their advantage and make better investment decisions.

3

THE SURPRISING TRUTH

> *Reaching any goal in trading requires specific domain knowledge and technical skills. But then, after that, it's all mindset management. Yet most people ignore that—they automatically think they have that last part all figured out, and it's a mistake.*

— YVAN BYEAJEE

Options have a long historical background, most of which may be undocumented since early literature points to the use of the principles of options as far back as Ancient Greece.

Options trading is no 17th-century phenomenon; in a second, you'd realize why options trading is a valuable skill to have, especially when you do not have large assets to profitably trade on the stock markets.

In his work "Politics," Aristotle describes an earlier philosopher, Thales of Miletus (624–546 BC), a Greek philosopher and mathematician who used options to secure the rights to olive presses. Here is how the story goes: Thales had spotted an opportunity in the olive business but, like most others in the same profession, didn't have enough capital to hire olive presses. However, this was a risky idea in an uncertain market. Thales proposed that he could make a "down payment" to secure the olive presses on the grounds that if the olive harvest proved bountiful, he'd hire the presses at the agreed price. The harvest period came, and Thales' intuition proved correct. The demand for presses increased, so he hired the presses at agreed-upon prices and rented them out at an even higher price. He reaped great profits from this trade!

Important elements in this tale include Thales' lack of capital, his intuition, the down payment, and the higher prices he rented them out for. These elements are the core framework of options even today. Wow!

THE 17TH CENTURY DUTCH TULIPS DEBACLE

Options weren't an economic phenomenon until the early 17th century when they were first used in their primitive forms. During the early 1600s, tulip bulbs had become a luxurious commodity in the Dutch economy and had gained popularity in the worldwide market. Tulip farmers had discovered a way to produce the tulip faster by vegetative means. The traditional method took 12 years to fully mature, while the vegetative method only took the tulip a year. This created a tulip frenzy in society, with everybody bidding on increasing the value of the flower. An increase in popularity also led to a dramatic rise in demand, which further caused the prices of tulip bulbs to skyrocket. Everyone wanted to jump on the tulip bandwagon; some middle-income folks sold their entire fortune for the fear of missing out. However, speculations were not all in favor of the coming harvest. This means some people were hopeful that the prices would continue to go up, others not so much. For some time, the market did okay; rich folks didn't have problems buying them. The average individual, however, couldn't afford it. So, they took the only way out, which was to take loans to purchase the option or make a "down payment." People continued to buy tulips on credit, hoping that the price would continue to rise.

Although everyone was excited about the new developments, there were two kinds of investors. The first group was those who anticipated a booming market and bought a type of option called call options that increased in value as the price of tulips increased. The second group included those who forecasted the plummeting prices of the tulip bulbs and purchased an option called put options that would increase in value as the price of tulips decreased. These options were sold to customers by the farmers. As markets continued to speculate, the demand for options increased, and so did the price of the options.

In 1638, the Dutch economy collapsed and quickly fell into recession. Production of tulips had come to a halt, demand for tulips dropped remarkably, and crops were going bad, causing the prices of the goods to plummet as well. Producers who'd sold options were unable to deliver on their obligations. This meant that folks who bought the options, specifically put options, lost not only the goods but the money paid for the options as well, even though their intuitions were correct (Roos, 2020).

Put option sellers were unable to pay up on the deal, leading to Holland and other customers being unable to *collect* their goods. This led the participating individuals to declare bankruptcy, causing the tulip markets to totally crumble.

OPTIONS IN TODAY'S MARKETS

In today's market, the fundamental principles aren't really dissimilar from what the Dutch practiced in 1600. Since the establishment of the New York Stock Exchange market and its regulating body, the Securities and Exchange Commission (SEC), the options market has become sophisticated and has seen rapid growth. It was formally made accessible to the public by the Chicago Board Options Exchange in 1973 and has continued to expand the market since then (Finnerty, 1978).

Options have become the go-to vehicle to hedge risk. Big hedge funds use options on large investments to mitigate risk in case market prices don't go as expected. Considering how options are utilized, think of them as a sort of *insurance* traders use to protect their portfolios from catastrophic losses in the event of market downturns or crashes.

THE BENEFITS OF OPTIONS TRADING

Are there any other benefits to trading options besides the *insurance* they provide? Certainly. Options are advantageous in the following ways:

Less Financial Commitment, High Returns, and Lower Risk

Options have the potential to generate high returns at a faster rate compared to buying the underlying stocks themselves and have limited risk exposure. For example, let's assume you have a capital of $10,000 and anticipate that the value of a particular stock will go up. The stock is currently trading at $90 per share. If you buy 100 shares of stock at $90 per share, you have to invest $9,000. Let's say your predictions were right, and the price shoots up to $120. This means you can sell the stock for a profit of $3,000.

$$(\$120 - \$90) \times 100 \text{ shares} = \$3,000.$$
$$\$3,000.00 \text{ represents an ROI of}$$
$$(\$3,000/\$9,000) \times 100 = 33.33$$

Let's see how that scenario plays out for options.

Let's assume you want to buy an at-the-money call option that expires in 60 days, giving you time for your prediction to play out. You would therefore purchase a $90 call option that expires 60 days in the future. On average, the option would cost you $5.00 (Don't worry—we will explain all the option terminology and pricing components in a later chapter.)

Options are bought and sold with contracts, with each contract consisting of 100 shares. If you bought one contract for 100 shares, your total investment to control those 100 shares would be $500! ($5.00 option premium x 100 shares). No matter what happens to the stock, your total risk is just $500 versus the $9,000 paid for buying the stock.

If, on or before expiration, the stock moves to the same $120 price, your $5.00 call option may be valued as high as **$21.00***. Your profit is $16 per option x 100, or $1,600 – a 320% profit.

You basically risked only $500 to make $1,600.

If you bought two contracts, your total investment would be $1,000 to make $3,200, which is $200 more than buying the stock.

***Note**: Options prices increase as the underlying security increases in value. We will discuss the term Delta, which is an expression of how much the option increases in value with each $1.00 rise, in a later chapter. For this example: An at-the-money option usually has a delta of .50%, meaning that it gains $.50 in value for each $1.00 rise. As the stock continues to rise, the Delta keeps increasing as well. We just estimated that with a $30 increase in the stock, the option would capture about 70% of the total move.

Opportunity in Any Market Condition

Options trading is like a box of chocolates—it can bring benefits in any market condition! When the bulls are charging, options can help amplify returns and ride the wave of upward momentum. If the bears come out to play, options can act as a shield, protecting against potential losses and protecting existing investments. And when the market gets all wild and unpredictable, options can be used to trade volatility and profit from sudden price movements, regardless of market direction. Even when the market is slow and steady, options can provide opportunities for income generation through the sale of options. With its versatility, options trading can be a valuable tool for investors in any market condition.

THE RISK OF OPTIONS TRADING

Along with the wonderful benefits of trading options, like anything, there are risks:

High Volatility and Fluctuating Option Prices: In times of high volatility, either up or down in the markets, options prices can have dramatic swings versus the price of the underlying stock. Market Makers price options in proportion to perceived risk.

- Time Decay: Options have a set expiration date. Time decay erodes the options' price the closer the options get to expiration. In these cases, and especially with short-term options, the options could be rapidly decreasing in value while the underlying security is moving in the investor's favor.
- Limited Life Span: All stock options are expiring assets. You can buy options for the day or buy them expiring two years from now. However, on expiration day, they expire, and if the option has not moved in your desired direction, you lose your investment. Stocks never expire, and you only lose your investment when you sell them.
- Limited Liquidity: Some options may have lower trading volumes and be illiquid, making buying and selling harder.

What Are the Requirements for Approval to Trade Stock Options?

Trading stock options requires meeting certain requirements set by the brokerage firm. Each brokerage firm has its own requirements, and traders need to check with them. In general, investors must have a margin account, apply for options trading privileges, maintain a minimum balance, and possibly complete additional training or education programs.

These requirements are necessary to ensure that investors are equipped with the essential knowledge and financial resources to manage the risks involved in options trading.

4

THE UPS AND DOWNS, INS AND OUTS OF OPTIONS

 *Luck is a preparation meeting opportunity.*

— OPRAH WINFREY

To succeed in options trading, it's crucial to have a thorough knowledge of the terminologies and strategies involved in options trading. Ignorance in the options market, or any market for that matter, can result in significant losses. A huge part of being a successful trader is the ability to identify opportunities and use them. To do that, you need information and the ability to interpret that information. In this chapter, we'll cover key options trading terms with examples to get you started.

THE LANGUAGE OF STOCK OPTIONS TRADING

The terms in this section describe various concepts associated with options trading.

Types of Options

There are two main types of options: call options and put options.

Call options give you the right, but not the obligation, to buy the underlying security at a specific price on or before its expiration date. Put options, on the other hand, give you the right but not the obligation to sell the underlying security at a set price on or before their expiration.

Options are contracts that give their holders the right, but not the obligation, to buy or sell an underlying asset.

To understand how call and put options work, consider a scenario where you have an interest in Tesla stocks. After conducting your research, you believe that Tesla's stock price, trading at $181.41, will drop to $100 in a week. To take advantage of this expected price movement, you purchase a *put option*, giving you the right to sell the Tesla stocks at $181.41 even if it is trading $100 lower. This means that while others are selling their Tesla stocks for $100, you can sell yours for $181.41.

There are other ways to take advantage of a price movement like this and make a profit. In fact, you'd mostly find that options tend to be minimal-risk instruments when compared to other types of derivatives.

Now suppose you expect the value of Tesla stocks to rise above $181.41 in a week. You would take advantage of this by buying a *call option* at a specified strike price and expiration, which will increase in value as Tesla stock rises.

Which is better, buying the stock or the option? There's no standard answer.

Would you get a call option instead of just buying Tesla shares and selling them later at a profit? The simple answer is that it costs more to buy shares outright. Tesla is trading at $181.41, and you believe it will rise in the weeks or months to come. One way to capitalize on this movement is to buy 100 shares of Tesla at the current market price of $181.41. This investment costs $18,141.

Another way is to purchase an at-the-money call option that is near the current stock price and expires in 90 days —giving ample time for the movement. Let's just say that option costs $30.40, so the total investment for one contract—100 shares—is $3,040. This requires significantly less of an investment.

So, which is better: Buying the stock or the option? There is no standard answer; both have their pros and cons.

The pro for stock purchases is that you own an asset—100 shares of stock—that never expires. The con is that if prices move down, it is worth less, leaving you with two options: Either sell at a loss or hold on to the stocks, hoping they move back up.

The pro for the option is that it ties up a lot less cash. The big con for the option is that it will expire, and if the stock does not move in the anticipated direction, then you lose all or part of the $3,040 investment.

With the option, your risk is limited to what you paid, and that is it.

Stock Options Definitions

Stock options market terms you need to know include:

- **Options contracts:** Typically, a contract defines the agreement held between two or more parties. An options contract facilitates a possible transaction between the writer or seller of the option and the buyer to trade an underlying asset at the strike price.

- **Strike price:** The price at which you'll buy or sell the underlying stock, depending on the contract you have purchased.

- **Premium:** The price paid to buy or sell an option at a given time, similar to a down payment. It gives you the right to exercise the option to trade at a later date. This is effectively the price of the option contract.

- **Expiration time:** The expiration time, as defined based on the type of option, is the day and exact time that a particular option's contract will expire. At expiration, both parties involved lose the right to buy or sell their options.

- **Intrinsic value:** When there is profit to be made from exercising an option whereby there is a positive difference between the strike price and the market price of the underlying security, the option contract is said to have intrinsic value. For example, if a stock is trading at $100 and you buy a $90 call option, its intrinsic value is $10.00.

- **Extrinsic value:** Refers to the difference between the premium of an option and its intrinsic price or value. In the example above, if the price of the $100 call option was $11.00, there is $10 of intrinsic value and $1.00 of extrinsic value, otherwise known as time value. The longer the time value of the option, the more the price of the option will rise.

- **Underlying:** The security whose performance affects the value of the option contract. If you bought a Tesla option contract, the underlying asset is Tesla stock.
- **Exercise:** The act of fulfilling the options contract by buying or selling the underlying security at the agreed price.
- How far away the expiration date of an option is will have an impact on its pricing. Options that are closer to their expiration date will cost less than options that are further away. As discussed, a long-dated option will have a higher premium because of the extra time value.
- **In-the-money (ITM):** A term used to describe an option that has intrinsic value, meaning its strike price is above the underlying for a put option and below the underlying for a call option.

For example, if a call option gives you the right to buy an underlying stock at $100 and the stock is trading at $130, the option is said to be in the money because of the profitable difference between the strike price of $100 and the price of the stock at $130. The option holder could buy shares at $100 and sell them at $130, making a profit.

- **Out-of-the-money (OTM):** An option that has no intrinsic value and would conceivably result in a loss if exercised immediately. They are the opposite of ITM. In the example above, an out-of-the-money call on a $130 stock is anything above $130.
- **At-the-money (ATM):** An option that has a strike price equal to the current market price of the underlying security.
- **Call option:** A contract that gives the holder the right but not the obligation, to buy the underlying security at the agreed strike price.
- **Put option:** A contract that gives the holder the right but not the obligation to sell the underlying security at the agreed strike price.
- **Implied volatility (IV):** The general movement of the underlying based on market activities and forecasts.

The volatility of the underlying is an important measure because the more volatile the underlying, the higher the likelihood of it moving in our favor. That is why the more volatile the underlying asset, the more the option will cost.

Option Periods

Stock options contracts are only valid for a limited time, and this varies based on your trading goals as defined by the contract. Before buying any stock options contract, it is crucial to understand its duration. These are the following ways to categorize stock options by duration:

Monthly: Stock options with regular monthly expiration dates have a period of one month, two months, or three months. While weekly options expire every Friday, monthly options expire on the third Friday of each month. Although called monthly options, options in this category can have expiry cycles ranging from three months to nine months. Furthermore, given the period, monthly options have a more costly option contract compared to weekly options because of their longer time value.

Weekly: Weekly options behave like monthly options, except they are only valid for eight days. They become available and active every Thursday, after which they expire eight days later, on the next Friday. Unlike monthly options, weekly options offer more frequent trading opportunities—52 times a year. Also, in most cases, trading strategies typically used for monthly options can be applied to weekly options. Other properties of weekly options include:

- Smaller premiums: This is due to the shorter expiration dates of the options. Options with a longer expiration date have greater premiums.
- More volatile: Since the weekly time frame is smaller than the monthly, it is prone to high volatility, responding to changing price levels at higher rates.
- Higher time decay rate: Option contracts lose value over time due to the passage of time. The rate of loss in value of the options contract is called *time decay.* The closer an options contract period gets to the expiration date, the greater the rate of loss of value.

Special Note: Even though weekly options have smaller premiums, we get to sell them 4 times a month! And time decay becomes our best friend!

Long-Term Equity Anticipation Securities (LEAPS): Option contracts that last for more than one year are referred to as LEAPS. It's a no-brainer to guess that their premium is also higher compared to standard options, such as monthly options and weekly options.

Volatility: Market prices always fluctuate; volatility describes fluctuations in the prices of an underlying asset in the options market.

Time value: How much time remains until an option contract expires is referred to as the time value of the option. It is also referred to as extrinsic value.

5

WHY WEEKLY OPTIONS?

> *The goal of a successful trader is to make the best trades. Money is secondary.*

— ALEXANDER ELDER

Weekly options trading, also called "weekly," refers to option contracts that are valid for a week. Although options trading began back in the 1970s, weekly options made their first appearance on the Chicago Board Options Exchange (CBOE) in 2005; however, options during that era were based on index options (National Association of Securities Dealers Automated Quotations, 2021).

The availability of options was very limited and only traded by a few companies. Five years later, the CBOE announced another set of weekly options based on four exchange-traded funds (ETFs). In the same year, on June 25, 2010, the CBOE introduced more weekly options on four individual equities: Bank of America (BAC), US-listed shares of BP, Apple (AAPL), and Citigroup (C). Having grown in popularity, different kinds of assets— equity, index, company stock, and so on—from different companies were added to the CBOE weeklies.

Weekly options are similar to monthly options. The primary difference is the days-to-expiration (DTE). Since days-to-expiration are shorter for the weekly option, why would we want to trade weeklies?

4–5 Times the Number of Trades as a Monthly Option Seller

In contrast with monthly options, the nature of weekly options makes it an efficient, fast-paced market. The availability of trades on a weekly basis automatically allows the trader to make up to four times as many trades as a monthly trader. Moreso, because traders can make profits or cut losses quickly, weekly options provide the potential for traders to maximize profits or cut losses.

Here's a practical example using Charles Schwab (SCHW). At the time of writing this, SCHW is trading at $58.17. If we suspect the market prices will remain in an uptrend, we could sell a weekly at-the-money put contract for $1.20. If the market trend is positive the next week, we rinse and repeat, selling another put option and banking the premium immediately.

We do this for 4 weeks to make $1.20 x 4 x 100 shares = $480 per contract.

Let's compare that with the monthly alternative. The put sells for $2.62 x 100 shares = $262 per contract.

We make 83% more selling the weeklys, with a profit of $218 per contract!

Lower Premiums

Since weekly options have a shorter time frame than monthly options, the premiums for these options are generally lower. This makes it more accessible for traders who want to enter the options market with a smaller investment. However, never forget that we get to sell these options four times a month!

Better Risk Management

With weekly options, traders can more precisely manage risk exposure, moving in or out of highly liquid positions as events dictate. This allows for more flexibility in adjusting to changing market conditions.

Hundreds of Stocks with Weekly Options

Since 2010, hundreds of the best companies have offered weekly options, so there is ample opportunity. It is important to note that companies themselves do not offer options. There are regulatory concerns ranging from low stock pricing to limited trading volume, making options illiquid. However, the best of the best all have weekly options and trading volumes are high.

Increased Liquidity

As weekly options have become more popular, the trading volume and liquidity of these options have increased significantly. This can be beneficial for traders looking to enter and exit positions quickly and easily.

Ability to Trade the News

Weekly options allow traders to take advantage of upcoming news or events that may impact the underlying stock. This can provide opportunities for profits, as traders can place short-term trades based on their analysis of the expected impact of the event.

6

SIMPLE WEEKLY STRATEGIES

> *Games are won by players who focus on the playing field, not by those whose eyes are glued to the scoreboard.*
>
> — WARREN BUFFETT

Before we jump into selling options, allow me to walk you through what a strategy is and the framework upon which I built my strategy.

A trading strategy, as defined by the Corporate Finance Institute, "is a fixed plan for buying and selling securities designed to generate a profitable return on the investments" (Park, 2021). We will discuss this further in a later chapter about how and why you need to develop a trading plan.

Briefly, having a trading plan with rules and guidelines takes the emotion out of trading. If an event happens, positive or negative, you have a plan in place, and you just execute it. The plan details your level of risk, so you can sleep worry-free in any market.

If you have ever awakened in a sweat and had great anxiety about the performance of a position, you have way too much invested with no plan. That is not healthy financially or emotionally.

Not every trade is going to be in your favor. Everyone makes what we call "a temporary investment" into someone else's account—a loss. One of my beliefs is that if you change your language, you can change your life. So the operative word for me is "temporary." As you will learn in a later chapter, the beauty of what we do can be rolled into next week.

WEEKLY SALES WINNING STRATEGY

As I said, my strategy is riding on a wave produced by the market. You cannot fight the market, which is 'pushed' about by large financial institutions. In any market, your goal is to swim with the wave, not against it. What happens when a surfer meets up with a rogue wave? They get off! Same with the market.

The basic principle for the WHY of selling weekly options is… drum roll…

80–85% of options are unexercised and worthless! Options were originally "invented" as protection for large accounts. They are basically like buying Home Owners Insurance.

If an institution or an individual had a large position, they could buy put insurance to protect them in a sudden downturn. This was really effective for large institutions because they could preserve their profits. In those cases, they did not care if they lost their investment because their goal was to protect profits. And as you will discover, there are ways the fund could sell options, either monthly or weekly, to help pay for this insurance. Wouldn't it be nice to do that with health or auto insurance?

It is important to note that of the 80–85% of options expiring worthless, many were either calls or puts that were bought because of a directional bias. You believe a stock is going up, and you buy a call to profit. Or you believe a stock is going down, and you buy a put to profit as well.

In these scenarios, option expiration and time decay may not be in your favor. If you believe a stock is going up over a given time frame (or down), you buy the call or put.

There are several possible outcomes:

- The stock moves in your direction, the options become very profitable, and you take profits.
- The market moves against you, the option loses value, and you exit with a loss.
- The market remains flat to sideways and does nothing, letting time decay and erode the value of the option. Even though the stock may move in our favor, you have a loss.

An option buyer has a 1/3 chance of making a profit! An option seller has a 2/3 chance of making a profit!

What Would You Rather Be—An Option Buyer or Seller?

There is no right or wrong. Many option buyers make very large profits because they understand the risks and have the knowledge to ride the trends. For consistent income, sleep-at-night insurance, and creating your personal ATM, option selling is the ticket.

Time Decay Is Our Best Friend

An important component of an options contract is time decay, which is the gradual or exponential loss in value of an option as it approaches its expiration date. Remember, options have a time value that is factored into the pricing of the option—it's why weeklys are cheaper than monthlies in the first place. With each passing day, the time value of the option diminishes, which means the value of the option also declines.

Also, the rate of time decay is proportional to the time left until the option expires. In other words, time decay is gradual; the farther away the option is from the expiration date, the more gradual the time decay. Theta is a measure of the rate at which time passes. This rate increases the closer the choice is to its expiration date.

TIME DECAY IS CRITICAL TO OUR TRADING STRATEGY

Selling weekly options in our KaChing Method, outlined in an upcoming chapter, has two elements of time decay that work in our favor. First, we select a stock, and we *buy* a long-dated put that expires in 90 to 120 days. That is our "insurance." Next, we sell a weekly put that meets our objectives and expires in 8 days (assuming we buy on a Thursday for the following Friday's expiration). If the market moves up, sideways, or even down a little bit, depending on what strike price we sell, time decay erodes the price of the option and accelerates our profits. At the same time, we have our long-dated insurance put (don't worry, *all* this is explained), and as the market moves up or stays sideways, the time decay is a lot less because of the long expiration date.

So, what does a short-term put with faster time decay mean when paired with a slow-time decay—long put?

Profits!

7

THE WEEKLY CASH KACHING FORMULA

> *Don't ever make the mistake of believing that market success has to come to you fast. Trade small, stay in the game, persist, and eventually, you'll reach a satisfying level of proficiency.*
>
> — YVAN BYEAJEE

I am excited to present this chapter because it is at the heart of what we do. Extracting weekly profits requires a specific skill set. Once you understand and learn it, you can use your mind and an internet connection to generate income from wherever you are in the world!

The basic setup is as follows:

- Step 1: We select a stock we want to trade and start a relationship with (more on that in another chapter).
- Step 2: We **buy** a long-dated put option that expires in approximately 120 days and past the next earnings announcement. This is our sleep-at-night insurance.
- Step 3: We **sell** a short-dated put that expires the following week. That premium is instantly credited to your account.
- Step 4: Manage, rinse, and repeat.

Recall Theta—Option Time Decay?

As outlined in the previous chapter, Theta is a measure of option time decay. For option sellers, time decay plays a key role in the success of our strategy:

- Long-dated insurance puts have slow decay because there is so much time before they expire. It is usually slow until the option has less than 30 days to expire—then it speeds up.

- The short-dated puts we sell for weekly income decay fast—in seven days, since we want to keep all the options premium, the faster the time decays, the better.

WHY ARE SELLING OPTIONS LIKE WINE AND ICE CREAM?

When a restaurant buys a bottle of wine, they pay X dollars and sell four glasses for Y dollars for profit.

A better analogy is ice cream shops that buy a 5-gallon tub for, say, $50. Each tub has 100 scoops, and each of those scoops sells for $3 and up. So, they pay $50 and collect $300! Not a bad business model!

Our long-dated put is the tub of ice cream that lasts for 120 days; each scoop is the weekly put we sell.

Let's use Charles Schwab (SCHW) as an example:

SCHW is trading at $74.00

- We **buy** a $70 put expiring in 120 days and past the next earnings date for $4.20
- We **sell** next week's at the money 74 put and collect $1.28
- We have a tub of ice cream with 16 weekly scoops and the potential to collect $1.28!

- If you had 1 contract (100 shares), you would pay $420 for the insurance and collect $2048.
- If you had 5 contracts (500 shares), you would pay $2,100 for the insurance and collect $10,240.
- If you had 10 contracts (1,000 shares), you would pay $4,200 for the insurance and collect $20,480; this is $1,280 a week.

RISK AND NUMBER OF CONTRACTS

In the Trading Plan section, we address risk and how to put together a plan where you always feel safe and sleep well. There will be times when trades need to be adjusted, and we have a dedicated chapter for those adjustments.

For now, why did we choose the $70 put for protection versus something else? Now, there is no right or wrong way here; it is *all* about your risk threshold and understanding *exactly* what you are responsible for in case the trade goes haywire.

Risk Percentages

For me, I like to keep each trade at no more than 5% of my total portfolio, and most are at 3%. That means there is *never* a position that is going to tank my account!

In the example above, we have a $4.00 spread between the $74 short put we sold and the $70 long put we bought. The maximum exposure is $4.00, less the premium you took in that week of $1.28. If the market tanks, your risk is $2.72 per share.

- 1 contract (100 shares) is $272
- 5 contracts (500 shares) is $1,360
- 10 contracts (1000 shares) is $2,720

Account sizes and risk are near 3% (These came out to be 2.7%)

- $10,000 – 1 contract is $272 – 2.7%
- $30,000 – 3 contracts is $816 – 2.7%
- $50,000 – 5 contracts is $1,360 – 2.7%

If SCHW suddenly drops, the short put you sold is worth more because it is solidly "in the money"—meaning you sold a 74 put and now the stock is trading at $71. At the same time, your long-term insurance has risen in value to offset and keep your risk contained.

If you were to exit the trade, buying to close your short put and selling to close your long insurance put, the difference is the risk (plus or minus a little on some fees and timing differences).

Delta Method to Choose Your Long Put Insurance

- As outlined previously, Delta is a term used for options that measure how close the option price moves when the stock price moves.
- A 100% delta means that if the stock moves $1.00, the option price will move the same $1.00
- A 50% delta is 50%, and so on.
- The average delta in most of my long protective puts is 25%. For me, that offers enough protection if the stock has an edge and is performing. If any long put delta goes under 25%, I cash it out and buy another with the 25% delta. (A 25% delta means a 75% probability the option will expire worthless, which is what we want! The lower the delta, the higher the probability the option will expire worthless. Of course, less risk means less premium.)
- In "risk-on" times, and with a stock that continues to hold its own, I increase the delta to 35–40%. Sometimes that means a $2 to $3 spread. The risk is very contained. Yes, you pay more for the insurance; however, the premiums sold are greatly inflated and juicy because Implied Volatility (IV) is high. (High IV means higher premiums). When the market moves to

"risk-off," you can close that and select another strike with around a 25% delta.

WHAT STRIKE TO SELL FOR YOUR WEEKLY SHORT OPTION?

There is no one-size-fits-all here because risk and reward are different for everyone.

Technically, you collect the most premium at or near the money. In the SCHW case, the stock was bouncing around $74 and had been up and down a little for a while. For me, selling "at the money" was a good risk and reward. The short delta was 50%, meaning there was a 50/50 probability the trade would perform. However, when you add in the time decay, even between a Friday and a Monday or Tuesday, it seems to me that it improves the odds.

Many more conservative investors sell more out of the money. And that, of course, is fine. The trade-off is a premium. The $74 short put with a delta of 50% had a $1.28 premium. If you wanted a higher probability, then a 70 put with a delta of .27 (73% probability of success) has a premium of $.58, less risk, and 55% less premium. Or you could sell the 71 put for $.90 with a delta of .38 (62% probability of success) for $.90. That is 30% less premium.

This is all about risk versus reward and your personal preferences. For me, if the trend is moving along and up, the reduced risk does not offer that much more protection and is not worth losing 30–55% in premium.

Understanding Your Stock's Personality

You do not have to be a technical analysis guru to look at your stock with a few simple indicators to see where sellers are turning into buyers, and buyers are turning into sellers. There is an up and down for all stocks that have decent premiums.

Here Are My Basic Tools

- Moving averages—I use the 100, 50, and 20—just to keep track. Look at this over a 3-month time frame because we are selling premiums between earnings statements. Think of any KaChing as a 3-month trade.
- Price Action and Volume—just seeing the daily buying and selling. If the stock moves up to a resistance level, it may pull back a little as traders take profits. If I saw that trend, I would sell slightly out of the money, collect a little less premium, and allow for the move. If there is a

down day on low volume and no news, it is just some profit-taking.

- On the other hand, after that little profit taking pull back, if green buying volume comes in, I may take a few contracts and sell an in-the-money put —in this case, maybe the $75 or even $76 to collect a big premium and watch the stock move up.

- Keltner Channels or Bollinger Bands: All trading platforms have these tools to determine the level of volatility and price trend. Look at charts over a few periods—1 year, 6 months, or 90 days—and you can see that as the stock moves up to the upper band, it may pull back historically for some profit-taking before moving back up. You can see historically what happens when the stock is in the lower band. How many times did buyers come in, and it moved up, or did it break through and set a new low?

Do not have many indicators and clutter up our chart! In my early days, I had so many that it was hard to see the actual stock! If there was one set of indicators that always worked, everyone would be using them! For me, I use moving averages for short-term trends, price action and volume for truth, and various time-frame views of the channels to make sure you see the whole picture.

Lastly, I am not doing any fundamental analysis, like looking at valuation, company earnings, or anything like that. The reason is that the market has priced all this into the stock price and chart. Microsoft, Apple, Schwab, City Bank, Adobe, Netflix, and on and on are brand names. We discuss this further in the Best Stocks for the KaChing Method chapter.

Potential Assignment

Once anyone sells a put, they can be "assigned" at any time, no matter what the price. This can't happen during the trading day, only after hours. In most cases, there must be a value proposition for someone to request to take the shares. If a $74 put was sold and the stock is now trading at $72, then that person may opt to get the shares at $74, well above the current market price of $72. However, if there is still a lot of time value left that is near or around $2.00, then there is really no benefit. Still, sometimes shares will be assigned. It may be someone settling their account or estate or leaving for an extended time and just wanting the stock.

Even if this were to happen, you would get the shares assigned to you and the funds taken out of your account. You can sell these immediately and then sell your insurance for a profit, and your total risk is the difference between the spread price ($4.00 less the premium collected). In a small account with not enough cash to buy the stock, the broker will make an automatic exercise trade to sell the shares and the put at the same time.

Trading can seem hair-raising, but there are easier ways to do it: Carefully planning out your strategy such that you don't end up pacing the room after placing a trade or joining the day traders who lost $1 billion dollars last year. The most important factor that contributes to the humongous losses reported in the news is overexposure to risk. The average trader plays the game like the lottery, expecting to make a huge sum at once. My weekly KaChing strategy is built for sustainability; little drops of water make the mighty ocean—little weekly profits can quickly pile up before you know it.

8

WHY WE SLEEP AT NIGHT WITH NO WORRIES

Investments are not a lottery; if it feels like the lottery, stay away from it.

— NAVED ABDALI

If there is ever a time when you can't sleep and are feeling anxious because of your positions in the stock market: You are overexposed. It's time to reduce your level of risk.

In any day trading training, the first lesson is deciding what your level of risk is per day. In other words, how much can you lose and emotionally say "Oh well" versus "OH NO!" If you went out for a nice dinner with your significant other and had some nice wine and a great meal, that could cost $200 to $250. Knowing that $250 is your threshold, the number of shares you bought for trade, along with your set stop loss, would prevent you from losing more than your risk.

This is not our focus; however, if you thought that SCHW was going up and wanted to trade it for a day, you would be taught to find how much a stock moves on average during a 5-minute period. If that was $.25, then you could buy 1,000 shares with a stop loss set at $.25 below the entry price. If the stock went down, you would "make a temporary investment into someone else's account," i.e., a loss and the max would be about $250.

If you took this trade without the stop loss protection, it may go down $1.00 or more, maybe move up again, and then back down, and you may end up losing a **lot** more. And if you say to yourself, "I wanted to own this stock anyway," you are not facing reality.

In our weekly KaChing formula, we are never without or long put protection, so we are always covered.

Here is an example for Chewy (CHWY) (*Note: This may make more sense after reading the Trade Adjustments chapter*):

CHWY is a brand-name pet retailer that got smashed in February 2021 and has been recovering. Although CHWY was risky, I had traded it for some time, and I saw a consolidation pattern at a support level, so to reduce my cost basis on the assigned shares, I put on a KaChing trade.

TRADE SUMMARY

Initial—CHWY at $36.22

- I had 2000 shares assigned, so each week, I sold 20 contracts.
- The initial long put was 20 $25 Put ($9,193).
- The collected put premium over 7 weeks was + $11,635 (this included ($3,500), where I rolled the loss into the following week, and CHWY bounced back (explained in Trade Adjustments).
- CHWY trading at $42.28: For better protection, I cashed out of the $25 Put for a loss of ($4,556) and bought 20 of the $35 Put ($7,500).
- Continued to collect premiums included in the total of $11,635 above.
- CHWY rose pre-earnings to $49.64 and was getting risky. I cashed in the $35 put with a loss of ($2,250) since it had a lot of time premium left.
- Bought 20 of the $45 put to get past earnings and have a tighter spread.
- CHWY tanks from $49.64 to $38.21: That is not good!

- Bought to close 20 of the short puts for the current week for a loss of ($6,838)
- Ouch!
- Sleep at night long-puts to the rescue! My $45 protective puts rocketed in value for + $10,036 profit – negating the loss in the previous week.

Net during these 7 volatile weeks was +$8,027 or $1,146 in cash per week. This took $4.00 off my base.

THE LESSON

What I want to hammer home is that if you are always protected with the proper long put, disaster will not strike. Also, even though you have a cash outlay for the long puts, they just don't decrease in value overnight. Their time decay is slow, which works in your favor. Most of the time, I close out the long put 30 days before expiration. The reason is that the closer to expiration, the faster the time decays.

ANOTHER REASON WE SLEEP WELL AT NIGHT: MULTIPLE, SMALLER POSITIONS TO HEDGE RISK

If each position is 3–5% of your portfolio, you can have many smaller positions spread out over different sectors and stocks. A diversified portfolio hedges risk. In our example, I used Schwab (SCHW), which is in the Financing and Banking sector. Even though I like that sector, I am not loading up on other companies because if the sector trades down for some reason, all the stocks will probably go down.

Along with SCHW, depending on sectors and trends, I will have other choices, maybe in Cloud Computing, Energy, and Ecommerce.

If you subscribe to IBD, Investor's Business Daily, you can see all the sector lists, what sectors are hot, and the leaders in those sectors.

Imagine trying to power a turbine against the wind's direction; that's a waste of energy. Not adjusting your strategy to the 'windy' market conditions will set you up for losses. The primary difference between a successful trader and an amateur is the ability to cut losses quickly. Professional traders have a plan and are ready to alter certain parameters of their strategy to accommodate the change in the direction of the markets. Please always keep this in mind. You're not the genie of the options market; no one is.

9

TRADE ADJUSTMENTS

I have a personal mantra that says, "I am in the right place at the right time, and things mostly work out fine." Of course, not everything goes completely according to plan. Markets go up and down, and outside global forces have an impact on our markets, news, etc. Sometimes we must make adjustments.

All adjustments are based on whether the stock still has an edge that makes it a good KaChing candidate. If that edge is lost, then we are out.

First and foremost: Keep a Journal to record all trades

I can't tell you how important it is to keep a journal; many people trade and, other than looking at their accounts, have no idea if they are making money! There are spreadsheets you can use, or you can do a manual journal in a notebook.

In a manual journal—see example—it is simple.

- Stock name
- Date of first entry
- Next earnings date (do not forget this)
- Long put information – strike price paid, and I like to put the total cost – like $2,000 if I bought 5 contracts (500 shares) of that put for $4.00.
- Each short put sale gets recorded as you put on the trade – say expiring 8/26 – SCHW 5 $74 puts @ $1.28 - $640
- At the end of the week, I mark the result – if it expired, then I enter $640 in green ink. If the stock pulled back a little but was still profitable and I got to keep $400 – then enter that. If the trade went against me and I had to buy the $74 put back for say, $2.00 – I enter the temporary loss for the week in red ink – in this case, since I kept the $1.28 and had to pay $.80 to close (-$400)
- Next is to enter what I sold for the next week. Let's say this was just some profit-taking; I may turn around and sell the $74 again. There is a good chance, since Implied Volatility is probably high that the premium I sell in for next week is

near or above the original $1.28 and totally offsets the $.80 loss per share from last week!

Here is an example. If you would like this tracker, please email us at info@kachingweeklyoptions.com and we will send it out.

KaChing Tracker										
TICKER	CHWY			NEXT EARNINGS DATE						
# CONTRACTS	10									
Long Puts										
Date Purchased	Expiration Period	Price of Stock	Strike Purchased	Premium Bought	Exit Premium	Premium Earned	Profit (Loss)	Cumulative Profit (Loss)	%	Trading Actions
09/23/22	1/20/2023	38.42	35.00	3.56	1.86	($1.70)	($1,700.00)	($1,700.00)	-47.8%	
Short Sold Puts										
Date Purchased	Expiration Period	Price of Stock	Strike Purchased	Premium Bought	Exit Premium	Premium Earned	Profit (Loss)	Cumulative Profit (Loss)	%	Trading Actions
09/30/22	10/7/2022	31.70	33.00	2.14	0.45	$1.49	$1,690.00	$1,690.00	79.0%	
10/07/22	10/14/22	35.89	34.50	1.04	0.28	$0.77	$766.76	$2,456.76	73.8%	
10/14/22	10/21/22	33.65	33.50	1.47	0.43	$1.05	$1,046.39	$3,503.18	71.0%	
10/21/22	10/28/22	36.98	34.50	0.63	0.05	$0.58	$583.38	$4,086.53	92.1%	
10/26/22	11/4/22	39.92	36.50	0.78	0.87	($0.08)	($83.50)	$4,003.03	-10.7%	
11/03/22	11/11/22	35.97	35.00	1.23	0.30	$0.93	$930.65	$4,933.68	75.4%	
11/11/22	11/18/22	39.15	37.50	0.84	0.13	$0.72	$716.76	$5,650.44	85.0%	
11/15/22	11/25/22	40.88	41.00	1.47	0.09	$1.38	$1,379.79	$7,030.23	94.1%	Net After Selling Long Puts
11/15/22	12/02/22	41.58	41.00	1.15	0.13	$1.03	$1,024.78	$8,057.01	89.0%	$6,357.01 9 weeks / $706 cash per week

Are you starting to see how this works? If the trade goes against us, we roll the loss into next week.

So, what are the steps to adjust?

Let's take Yeti (YETI) as an example. At the start, Yeti was at $87.24

We owned (5) 8/20/21 $85 puts @ $6.60 ($3,303). Earnings on 8/5/21. This is our long put.

$87.24 - Week 1 - 6/4/21 – sold (5) $86.50 @ $1.20 + $596.70 – net at close +$286 (Yeti traded down to about $86 and time value kept us profitable)

$85.96 Week 2 – 6/11/21 – sold (5) $85.50 puts @ $1.40 + $696.70 – net at close +$668

$93.89 Week 3 – 6/18/21 – sold (5) $92.50 puts @ $1.30 + $646.70. Yeti traded back down to $86, and we bought close @ $4.64 – net (-$1676)

$86.44 Week 4 – 6/25/21 – sold (5) $93 puts @ $5.60 + $2,796.69. Yeti jumped back up after profit-taking and got close to $93. We closed for a net of +$2,253

$91.88 Week 5 – 7/2/21 – sold (5) $93 puts @ $2.42 + $1212.75. Net at close + $1,163

$93.13 – Week 6 – 7/9/21 – sold (5) $94 puts @ $2.35 + $1,624.71. Net at close (286.59). Yeti traded down to $91.25

$91.25 – Week 7 – 7/16/21 – sold (5) $93 puts @ $3.20 + $1,596.69. Net at closing + $1,333.37

$89.32 – Week 8 – 7/23/21 – sold (5) $88 puts @ $1.60 + $796.72. Net at closing +618.42

$91.87 – Week 9 – 7/30/21 – sold (5) $92 puts @ $2.43 +$1,211.69. Net at closing +908.39

Total cash collected over 9 weeks was $5267, averaging $585 in cash/ week. I sat out the next week because of earnings, then sold at-the-money puts on 8/13/21 for + $883 and 8/20/21 for +$1,361.

Therefore, the total cash is $7511. The long put was closed out for (Remember— $2700—we bought those long puts for $3,303, so we recovered $603 due to slower time decay.) – net $4808. Average cash per week $437 or $1748 per month with just 5 contracts.

Discussion:

First, the difference between the amount of premium sold and the net at closing is because of the time value still left on the short put. If you are rolling early in the trading session on Friday, there may still be $.10 to $.20 or more of time value that the market makers are just leaving there to catch us and make us pay more if we must roll early. Usually, within 2 hours of market close, those premiums are really reduced.

During this period heading into earnings, Yeti was really bouncing around and mainly up, so I was comfortable selling at and a few times in the money. I could have easily backed off and sold the $92 put in Week 7 instead of the $93 and just collected less.

You can also see that for the two down weeks, selling the puts for the next week brought in more premium than I had to buy back the week before. Again, in Week 3, we sold the $92.5 for $1.30, and when Yeti pulled back, we had to buy it back for $4.64. We had a debit of $3.34 per share. If I had sold closer to the money in Week 4 and sold the $87 put, we would have collected maybe $1.50 or more, and it would just have taken another week to roll to erase the debit and be profitable. You can roll indefinitely as long as you have long put protection. This preserves your account value—even though you are buying to close at a loss one week, you are selling to open, and that premium offsets the loss.

That is the beauty of this system. If the stock still has an edge, you can keep rolling and banking premium until you are even or profitable.

A KACHING DOUBLE DIP

As you gain experience and confidence, there are times when a stock takes off, and you can sell twice in a week or roll into the next week.

In Yeti's case in Week 2: Yeti was trading at $85.96, and we sold the $85.5 put for $1.40. On Monday, Yeti rose to $93, and the delta of the short put was now about 15%, and more than 80% of the sold premium was in the bank. There was $.28 left (we sold it for $1.40).

The question to ask is, *Would you put on this trade for the next 5 days for $.28?* To me, it's a "no." Therefore, we cash those out and either sell the same week's 92 or 93 puts, and if the stock closes at, near, or higher, we get to keep most or all of the extra premium.

As a rule of thumb, if the short put delta is lower than the protective long put, then it is a candidate to roll early. This tactic can exponentially increase the size of an account.

If this happened on a Wednesday, my choice would be to roll the following week for extra time. If this was on a Tuesday, most of the time, the choice is the same week on Friday.

Final note: In the YETI example, there were two deltas KaChing Flips for a total extra cash of $1,785. I did not put them in the summary because it was confusing where those trades were coming from. That makes the total cash now $6,592 / $732 per week versus $437 per week. That is about 68% supersize.

This does not happen all the time! When the opportunities present themselves, and you take action, you are in the pro trader space.

10

THE BEST STOCKS FOR THE WEEKLY KACHING FORMULA

First, there is no one perfect stock, and each trader has their own preferences. In a perfect world, I would like stocks that show a steady upward trend and are not bottle rockets. If you have a trade on a certain stock, and suddenly it unleashes and blasts up $20–$30 or more, your long put erodes significantly, and you must adjust. On the other side, you are collecting all these juicy premiums and maybe even double-dipping (selling two short puts twice in the same week—explained in Adjustments). With a move like that, your spread between your long and short put maybe $20+, which is way past your risk threshold.

If you are okay with a wider spread and risk, you can keep selling to collect more premiums. In your Trading Plan, however, you state what your risk preferences are, so when faced with this decision, there is no "discussion." You know exactly what to do. During those times, I exit the long put, keep all the premium on the short put, and then decide if I still want to be in the trade.

If the stock is on fire, sometimes it is wise to let it take a breather for a week or so. Let the news or whatever propelled it settle down and allow the profit-takers to make profits. When it pulls back or gets on a more even trajectory, then redo the entire trade.

If I decide SCHW or any stock still has an edge, I can absorb losses, roll them over to the next week, and roll and roll until I am even or ahead. There are times when we lose the edge, and the stock makes a new low, and it is just time to step away. If we have been sticking to our Trading Plan, then we can absorb the temporary investment into someone else's account (loss) and find more profitable trades.

GOOD KACHING STOCK PARAMETERS

- It must be trading at $20 or higher. Under $20 stocks do not get any love from the big funds, so many times, the premiums are very low.
- Avoid stocks over $400—this is personal. The reason is that these stocks have their own personalities and can zoom way up fast, leaving

the long put in the dust or coming down harder for some profit-taking. Others trade these and are successful. This does not work for me.

- Avoid Apple. What? How can I say that? Apple is the most widely owned stock in the universe. When Apple goes on a tear, large hedge funds must liquidate because their holdings may exceed 5% of their fund. This requires a lot of paperwork. I own Apple stock, and it is great. I never made any consistent income trading it. As the legend Jim Cramer says, "Apple is a great stock to own but a lousy stock to trade."

- Avoid Chinese stocks (this is personal for me and may not apply to you). China has accounting transparency issues versus the strict requirements for US stocks and if the government takes a dislike to a company, anything can happen.

- ETFs, for the most part, do not have enough premium; however, you just have to look at them and see if anything makes sense. I have had several sustained trades with GLD–the gold ETF.

- It must show an up or sideways, consolidation pattern, meaning it is digesting and coiling for the next move. Look over a 3-month period since these are really 3-month trades.

For candidates, there are tons of websites. My personal favorite is Investor's Business Daily (IBD). For $34.95 a month, I can get their top 50, look at all 197 Industry Group Rankings, see how they rank, and see in what direction the rank is moving. Then look at the 33 sectors within the ranks for sector leaders. For example, a few months ago, the Energy Sector was rated very highly, and I found UNG and Devon Energy as sector leaders and put on some profitable trades.

CHART EXAMPLES OF GOOD KACHING CANDIDATES

Nutrien LTD (NTR)

Disclaimer: These are not trade recommendations and are shown for educational purposes only.

This is a daily chart for NTR. From September 2021 into May 2022 earnings, there was a nice period with general ups and downs that were suited for the KaChing Method. Even heading into May earnings, the acceleration provided excellent premiums. During this period, and depending on your risk tolerance, the long put would have been left in the dust and became too wide of a spread, so adjustments were needed.

Looking to the far right, if in a week or so, the sideways trend continues and NTR coils for another move, it could be a good trade candidate.

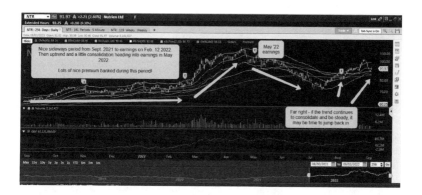

Diamondback Energy (FANG)

The same type of pattern. There were periods of chop, but there were some nice opportunities between November 2021 and May 2022. You would have exited in the middle of July as FANG reached a new 30-day low. If you had stayed in during this time, your long put would have protected you. Note – FANG does not have weekly options now. Nice chart example though.

DASH – Door Dash

DASH sold off after earnings earlier in the year, then consolidated along with the rest of the market. Then chugged along in a solid uptrend past earnings and beyond. This is very tradable.

EXAMPLES OF WHAT NOT TO LOOK FOR!

LGI Homes (LGIH)

Apple (APPL)

As we discussed, APPL is great to own over time and impossible to trade for the KaChing Method.

Applied Materials (AMAT)

AMAT mirrors the chip market at the time this was written. It is just too choppy to trade right now.

Finding the right market conditions is just one prerequisite to landing profits. People lose money even when trading in great market conditions. That's right! The big cheese of truly becoming successful as an options trader, or any other asset for that matter, is having a well-thought-out trading plan.

11

WHAT IS A TRADING PLAN AND HOW TO CREATE ONE

> *When a plan or strategy fails, people are tempted to assume it was the wrong vision. Plans and strategies can always be changed and improved. But my vision doesn't change. Visions are simply refined with time.*

— ANDY STANLEY

A stock and options trading plan is a blueprint for an investor that defines goals, risks, timeframes, and trading preferences. It is a written, unemotional guideline that takes emotion out of trading. When there is a market event that affects any given trade, if your plan is complete, you have a course of action, and all you do is execute. You do not think about it.

If you have ever held a stock or option position and wondered what to do (either sell to take profits or stop further losses), then you most likely do not have a plan.

Trading Plans can be complex or very simple, depending on who you are, your goals, etc. And you may have multiple plans: One for long-term holds in a core growth portfolio, another for an income growth portfolio or a retirement account, and another for more aggressive trading like intraday trading, swing trading, or options trading.

My options trading plan is very simple and has not altered much since it was first created.

Relative to trading Weekly options, it includes the following:

Capital Allocation

This is how much capital you are willing to deploy for this strategy. You can have a small account or a very large account allocation. The only difference is the size; the rest of the parameters (for me) remain the same. Let's say I am willing to allocate $50,000 to trade weekly options, and the maximum I will risk for each position is 3%, or $1,500. Furthermore, I only deployed $10,000 in capital for the week. The reason is that it keeps plenty in reserve, and there is never a risk of blowing up the account. That means I have, on average, 6–7 positions weekly.

Since we always have a long put and a short put, it means the width is the difference between the long and the short. For example, Stock A is trading at $50, and I sell an at-the-money $50 put for $.50. Our long-term protection is a $45 put. My risk is basically $5.00 for the spread difference, less the $.50 I collected for the premium, so $4.50. I could put on three contracts for this trade and be within my risk parameters.

Trading Goal

I plan my trading goals as follows:

- Minimum annual cash return of 25% (It is important to note that this plan, is not about portfolio growth, it is about spendable cash returns)
- 1/2 % per week on my trading account for each trade equals 26% annualized per year
- Taking the example above, collecting a $.50 premium on a stock trading at $50 is 1% for the week.

The message here is that, when broken down into these steps, this is *very* doable in an up-trending market. In this

$50,000 account, you could have up to 6–7 positions as defined above, each generating $250 to $500 a week in cash, $1,500 to $3,000 weekly, and $6,000 to $12,000 per month. How would that change your life?

If you have a more Risk On attitude, then increase the allocation. For me, the extra dry powder easily funds the ways to supersize what we discuss later and gives me peace of mind.

Types and Numbers of Positions

My dos and don'ts on a number of positions to trade include the following:

- The trend is my friend. If I feel the edge is still there in this trade, I stick with it. If a stock suddenly makes a new low with high selling volume, I am out.
- Never bulk up on too many trades in the same sector. I may love banks or consumer energy; however, spread the risk around and do not have all your eggs in one sector.
- I am willing to sit on my hands and hold cash during super volatile periods, like before a Federal Reserve meeting or some major world event or report.

- Never trade through earnings. I just take the chips off the table and enter 2–3 days again after all the buying or selling has taken place.
- In general, I favor lower contract positions to reduce risk even further. In other words, I will have more than 3–5 contract trades vs. 10 contract trades.

Profit Taking

My rules are the following:

- If I have 80% of the premium banked before the weekly expiration, I take it. Sometimes Friday to Friday can seem like an eternity. If I take in, say $600, and on a Tuesday or Wednesday, there is $480 in cash and that is over my weekly % goal, I bank it. Another way to look at it is: I sold the put at $.60, and there is $.12 left. Would I put on this trade right now to make $.12 for the same expiration period? That is a no, so I am out. This frees up capital, and if you sold the following week a couple of days earlier, you would bank more premium.
- For super-volatile markets, I accelerate that to 40% to 50%. If things are nuts, then I am banking quicker and not holding.

- Never second-guess or look back. This is challenging for us all. We have a decent profit and take it, then the market pulls back a little, and we feel like geniuses. Next, it recovers, and the position rockets backup and would have expired worthless, giving a 100% profit. That's the way it goes. Over time, you will have a lot more cash to stick to your plan!

ASSIGNMENT RISK AND ROLLING TO NEXT WEEK OR AN EXIT

As mentioned earlier, once you sell an option, the stock can be returned to you at any time. In most cases, unless the underlying stock is now in the money, an assignment does not happen. And if it does; it's a big whoop! You have limited risk because of your long put, so you just sell the stock that has been put to you and then sell and take profits on the long put.

Avoiding Assignment

Most of the time, when stock was put to me, it happened when the stock was way in the money, and there was almost no time value left. That usually happens on a Thursday after the close, so I woke up Friday with the stock.

For me, I look at the current stock price and how many strikes in the money the option has at that time. For example, if a stock was $50 and I sold a $49 put, and now the stock is trading at $46, the owner may decide to exercise their option for me to provide the stock to them at $49.

In general, if the stock gets to Wednesday and has not been assigned, there is a high probability it will be because the time value is really decreasing. So, if I decide to stay in the trade, I just roll into next week.

In the example above, if I believe the stock drop is just some profit-taking or a little market chaos, I will buy back the $49 puts at whatever price, maybe $4–$5, and sell next week's $49 puts at about the same price, which may be higher depending on Implied Volatility. So, there is a cash out and a new cash-in that often covers the cash out.

If the market is in a little downturn or the stock has some news and is trading down on low volume (still keeping our edge of being in the stock), the best move is to sell 1–2 strikes down. In this case, you buy back the $49 and sell next week's $47 or $48. Your cash-out may not equal the new cash-in; however, repeating this for next week gets you profitable.

This is the beauty of selling options: You can just keep rolling, and as long as the stock maintains its edge, at some point, it bounces back, and you are even and profitable.

Track Everything

Make sure to keep a trading log with each trade's details. This can be a simple paper journal or a spreadsheet. Also, make a place for notes and comments, such as what the market was like and why you put on the trades you did, adjustments, etc., when I look at at my journals, it helps me understand what happened, so I can keep learning.

Sometimes you may be rolling early in the week for a double dip, and when you look back in a few months, it may not be obvious what happened.

When I first started, I had a simple note journal with each stock on a separate page. I had the price of the stock, some comments on *why*, and the next earnings date.

At the top was the long put number of contracts, the put price, and the total in brackets [$3,500]. Under that was Week 1, Week 2, Week 3, and so on, and each week I would record the Friday result. It was fun to look at the weekly KaChing and see how quickly the long put was paid off, and the rest profited!

Example of a Trade Journal

Here is a screen shot for a Trade Journal and Tracker. If you want this Excel Spreadsheet, just email info@

Your trade journal setup can be more elaborate to factor in other parameters. I recommend using tools like Excel or any spreadsheet software to keep records and automate things.

As you master the art of keeping journals, you'll develop the trading mindset—psychological instincts that influence your behavior to edge towards making profits, minimizing losses, and mustering control of your emotions.

12

YOUR TRADING MINDSET

> If you can meet with Triumph and Disaster and treat those two imposters just the same.
>
> — RUDYARD KIPLING

WHAT IS THE DIFFERENCE BETWEEN AN INVESTING MINDSET AND A TRADING MINDSET?

In simple form, an investing mindset is more focused on long-term growth and wealth-building, while a trading mindset tends to focus more on shorter-term opportunities to make profits in the market.

An investing mindset is focused on building a long-term diversified portfolio based on solid fundamentals that tell a good story and hold assets over time. Warren Buffett is the quintessential investor, having long-term positions in the many stocks he owns. Many long-term investors are more set and forget unless there is a major change in the company's circumstances. In market downturns, and still with a great WHY, the long-term investor may buy dips to add to their portfolio.

When you're in a trading mindset, you're looking for quick wins and faster profits based on market conditions. You move in and out of trades using various methods, including day trading, swing trading (a few days to a few weeks), buying or selling options, etc. For the most part, you are not taking a deep dive into a company's fundamental analysis; you are just looking at the current chart and seeing a trend that you believe is tradable, either up or down.

Developing a Trading Mindset

A stock trading mindset refers to the attitudes, beliefs, and habits that shape an investor's behavior and decision-making when trading stocks. It encompasses both the emotional and rational aspects of trading and involves having a clear understanding of one's goals, risk tolerance, and investment strategy.

A successful stock trader needs to be disciplined, patient, resilient, able to manage their emotions and avoid making impulsive decisions based on fear or greed. They must also be adaptable and able to adjust their trading approach in response to changes in the market.

Ultimately, a strong stock trading mindset involves a balance of confidence and humility, self-awareness and continuous learning, and a willingness to take calculated risks while also managing downside risks.

Managing Fear and Greed

The most powerful forces of failure are fear and greed. The majority of traders who lose out on a trade were either scared they were going to miss out on huge gains or were in profit but couldn't bring themselves to close out the trade, always wanting more. These emotions are causes that lead to the following effects:

- You overleverage your account and run the risk of blowing it up with a margin call if the market tanks.
- Holding on to a losing position and not cutting your losses to free up capital.
- Removing the measures put in place to minimize losses.
- You fall for the herd mentality and make snap buy-and-sell decisions based on what the talking heads are reporting. You suffer from

overconfidence. After a few winning trades, you start to believe the rules do not apply to you.

These emotions can get out of control, and you could lose your entire capital with one wrong trade. You cannot get rid of the emotions, but you can control them. You don't need to become a monk or some kind of guru to visit the temples of Sri Lanka and put them in check.

All you have to do is abide by the strategy you've already laid out, no matter what! Other measures to put in place include:

- Becoming aware that trading isn't a get-rich-quick scheme.
- Being comfortable with the KaChings that flow in your favor and those temporary investments in another account is a fact of life. Don't fear; you have a plan!
- Keep a detailed track of your trades; create a journal.
- Continue to empower your mind by studying. A true trader never stops learning. You are not your trades.

Don't beat yourself up during bad trades, and don't over celebrate during good trades, either. It is simply what it is: a flow. If you manage your risk as we have taught, then you have a huge trading advantage over other traders.

You are not a genius after a few winning trades, and you are not a loser after a few that did not go your way. Always see the whole picture in the market, your individual stocks, and your life. You make adjustments every day—maybe a different route to a destination based on traffic or a dietary choice based on a goal; it is the same in the market.

Trade the plan, and do not be afraid to sit on your hands and not trade when things are wonky out there!

Adjust Your Trading Plan as Your Confidence and Experience Grows

When I started day trading, my maximum daily loss tolerance was $100. Then it was $200, and it stayed there for quite some time. As my skills increased, so did my risk tolerance, and soon I was allocating $1,000 a day. If I managed to expend that in the day, I closed up shop no matter when it was, and walked away. It has been the same with the KaChing method.

WHAT MAKES A SUCCESSFUL TRADER

Master of Emotions

Successful traders have mastered the art of isolating their trades from any form of emotion. They aren't scared of losing money because they know it's a predefined risk they're willing to take. A professional protrader takes profit at the pre-defined price; even if there's the possibility of the market moving further than they expected, they'd still get out as planned. This way, they eliminate the consequences of greed and the influence of uncertainty.

Quickly Adaptable

Adaptability means not changing plans on a whim. NO! It's about knowing how to adjust your trade to fit into the ever-changing market structure. For example, let's say you intend to sell put based on an analysis of the previous assessment of the markets, and a sudden event occurs that changes the market structure. Would it be wise to still carry on with the initial plan? Of course not. Instead, you formulate a new plan that fits the current market conditions.

Always Improving Knowledge

Like with any profession, a successful trader is always learning on the job. The market is a zero-sum game; the folks on the other side of your trade are equally smart or smarter and are coming up with new ways to take your money. Hence, you should be constantly refining your strategy as well.

Keep to the Rules

If you've planned to enter at a certain strike price, do so. The moment you start to chase a trade or doubt what you are doing, you've already set yourself up for failure.

Understand the Personality of Stocks

Every stock has its own "personality," and over time, you get a feel for the possible swings. For example, many stocks pay high dividends quarterly. If the stock price has decreased, then the percentage payout will increase, and now a 4–5% dividend becomes irresistible to investors, and money pours in—it is like built-in support.

Others, like Apple, are hard to trade because, as we have discussed; when Apple is rising, many large funds have to sell because of the limits on ownership. Others, like Chewy and Schwab, often trade in patterns with their sectors and are also affected by sector rotation when the big funds reallocate their portfolios. Over time, these become familiar, and you can tell if the stock is down after a nice run-up that it is just a little profit-taking and nothing to worry about.

It is not an easy task to become a successful trader, but with the right mindset, the right strategy, and the proper implementation of your trading plan, becoming a successful trader will be easier than you think.

BONUS CHAPTERS

13

WAYS TO SUPERSIZE KACHING TRADES

> *When money realizes that it is in good hands, it wants to stay and multiply in those hands.*
>
> — IDOWU KOYENIKAN

There are ways to supersize your trades if market conditions are favorable. If you are trading in an uptrend and your weekly "paychecks" are flowing, then conditions are right. On the other hand, if you are adjusting your long put protection for a higher delta, then these trades have more risk because they are directional.

Buying a Long Calls

Often, in an uptrend, I buy a long call with the same expiration date as the long protective put. For example, if I am selling weekly puts on SCHW (Charles Schwab) and have my long put just after the next earnings release, I may buy a call that expires on the same date as my long put. This gives plenty of time for the trade to move in our favor.

Option 1: If SCHW was trading at $50, I would look to buy a strike with a delta close to .5, which is normally at-the-money and will move up $.50 for every $1.00 the stock rises. In this case, that would be a $50 strike price of $3.97. As SCHW rises in value, the delta is not static and will keep moving up with the stock. This is a good thing because it means that your call is increasing in value!

Option 2: If the trend is solidly up and again the market is in an uptrend, I may look at a call strike that is close to having the same intrinsic value and time value. Again, for SCHW trading at $50, that would be the $45 strike at $6.80 with a .7 delta. Yes, I am paying more for this strike; however, the delta now captures $.70 in value for every dollar increase.

For the $45 strike above, the intrinsic value was $3.92, and the Time Value was $2.94; that was as close to 50/50 as possible.

Option 3: If you *really* want to supersize, then look for a deep-in-the-money strike where the time value is just 1% of the stock price. In this case, the 1% is $.49, and that is a $27.50 strike at about $19.68 with a .94 delta.

There is no right or wrong, just the level of risk matched to our trading plan. For me, 99% of the time, I am selecting close to 50/50 between the Intrinsic Value and Time Value and am happy with a .7 delta.

Position Sizing

Again, I follow my trading plan and make sure that no one trade is greater than 3% of the portfolio. That keeps everything in balance. Also, just because I am selling 10 contracts of a weekly put and have 10 long contracts, I never buy 10 long calls, even if that was 3% or less. This is a pure directional risk with no hedge, so I will make 2–3 contracts and use them as a sweetener for the trade.

Bull Vertical Call Spreads

This is another option for someone who feels comfortable doing spreads. Spreads reduce your cost. For the SCHW example, you could buy the $50 call for $3.97 and, to hedge, sell the same expiration period $55 call and collect $1.87. Your final cost is about $2.10. The maximum profit on the directional call is infinity if the stock keeps rising.

On the spread, the maximum profit cap is $290 per contract. That is the spread width of $5.00 less the $2.10 cost to put on the trade. Break-even is about $52.10. The maximum loss is $2.10. Another option is to do this spread using monthly options, so instead of expiring in 6–9 weeks, it expires in 30 days. The pros are that you capture profits on an uptrend faster, and the cons are that there is less time for the trade to play out if there is a pullback. I like spreads because they manage risk well, and the profits are solid.

Exit Strategies

Directional trading is a double-edged sword. On the one hand, you want enough time to have the trade play out, and on the other, if there is a sudden pullback, what do you do? Back to your trading plan!

For me, on these spread trades, if I am down 35% at any given time, I am out and just take the loss. In the spread example above, the total cost of 10 contracts would have been $2,100, and 35% down is a minus $735 loss. I could easily absorb that and live to trade another day. Special note: The 35% is what I am comfortable with; it may be different for you. Trust your gut!

Math works out in your favor if you stick to your plan!

Say you have 10 trades with the same risk-reward ratio—the maximum profit is $290, and the maximum loss is $210 per contract. If you had 5 winning trades and 5 losing trades, your overall profit would be $400. You could be wrong 50% of the time and still make money. Even if you had four winners and six losers, the maximum loss is just $100. I would still want that $100; however, you are in good shape and can just trade on.

The big question here is: What is happening with the market or *you* if 50–60% of these trades are off? Sometimes it does happen when there is a giant pullback, like in March 2020 when COVID tanked the market. If there are no events, then take another look at the stocks, trades, and the reason for putting on the trade in the first place and recalibrate.

The Sudden Pop Back-up Remorse Syndrome

The market is volatile; that is an understatement. You may have had several trades where you stuck to your plan and exited, only to see the stock rocket back up, especially on high-beta (volatile) stocks. At the end of the month, you are not feeling so great because some or all of those trades became profitable. Regret creeps in, and self-doubt makes you start thinking you knew it was going to go back up, so why did you exit? Then the next time it happens, you let one slide, then another, and... you get hammered!

Getting paid to break the rules is the worst thing that can happen to you! Laugh it off because, at the end of the day, you made money on all the others. The above are my favorites because they are easy and not very complicated.

Outlined below are definitions of these terms and others, just for your awareness.

Advanced Strategies for Bullish Markets

Long Call Diagonal Spread

Let's say in June; a trader is bullish on a stock that is currently trading at $40 per share. The trader believes that the stock will gradually rise over the next few months. The trader decides to use a Long Call Diagonal Spread strategy by buying a longer-term October call option with a strike price of $40 that expires in 5 months for $3 per share and simultaneously selling an out-of-the-money July call with a strike price of $45 that expires in 1 month for $1 per share.

By selling the near-term call option for $1 per share, the trader is able to reduce the cost of buying the longer-term call option to $2 per share. The trader now has a net debit of $2 per share, which is the difference between the cost of the longer-term call option and the premium received from selling the near-term call option.

If the price of the stock gradually increases by $1 a month over the next 5 months and reaches $44 per share at expiration, the option would have an intrinsic value of $4 per share. If the traders sell monthly out-of-the-money options for $1 that expire worthless, then the total profit is $9 ($4 for intrinsic and $5 for expiring short calls). However, if the price of the stock does not increase or even decrease, the trader may experience a loss.

Bull Call Spread

A Bull Call Spread is another advanced options trading strategy that is used in a bullish market. This strategy involves buying a call option at a lower strike price and simultaneously selling a call option at a higher strike price. The goal is to profit from an increase in the under-lying asset's price.

The Bull Call Spread strategy is a good way to limit potential losses while still benefiting from a bullish market. By selling the call option with a higher strike price, the premium collected offsets the cost of buying the call option with a lower strike price. This reduces the cost of entry into the trade.

As always, there are risks involved with this strategy. If the underlying asset does not increase or decrease in value, the trader may experience a loss. Additionally, if the underlying asset's price increases too much, the profit potential may be limited, as the sold call option will be exercised, capping the profit potential.

Calendar Spread

Another advanced options trading strategy is a Calendar Spread (sometimes called a Horizontal Spread). This technique involves buying a longer-term option and selling a shorter-term option with the same strike price (unlike the Long Call Diagonal Spread, where the strike prices are different).

The Calendar Spread takes advantage of the difference in time decay between the two options. The shorter-term option will lose value more quickly over time, while the longer-term option will hold its value longer. By selling the shorter-term option and buying the longer-term option, you can profit from the difference in time decay.

If you're implementing a long call calendar spread, your goal is for the stock to be at or near the nearest strike price at expiration and to benefit from near-term time decay. Depending on where the stock is relative to the strike price, when you implement the strategy, you could have a neutral, bullish, or bearish outlook.

Iron Butterfly

An Iron Butterfly is an advanced options trading strategy that involves selling both a call option and a put option at the same strike price and buying a call option and a put option at different strike prices. This strategy is often used in a market that is expected to have low volatility.

If a stock is trading at $50 and you expect it to remain flat and close at $50 over a specified time period, then you would sell a $50 call and buy a $55 call, say for a net credit of $1.00. At the same time, you sell a $50 put and buy a $45 put, say, for another net credit of $1.00. If the stock is at or near the $50 strike, the maximum profit is the $2.00 in collected premium.

The Iron Butterfly strategy is useful because it allows traders to benefit from low volatility in the market while limiting potential losses. This is because the premium collected from selling the call and put options offsets the cost of buying the call and put options. If the underlying asset's price remains stable, the trader can benefit from the time decay of the options and profit.

Advanced Strategies for Bearish Markets

Long Put Diagonal Spread

A Long Put Diagonal Spread is the reverse of the Long Call Diagonal spread and is used by traders who are bearish on a particular stock or market. This strategy involves buying a longer-term put option at a higher strike price and selling a near-term put option at a lower strike price. The goal is to take advantage of the difference in time decay between the two options.

The Long Put Diagonal Spread is a flexible strategy that can be adjusted to suit different market conditions. It can be used to profit from a moderate decline in the stock price or to protect against a more significant downturn.

Bear Put Spread

A Bear Put Spread is another advanced options trading strategy used by traders who are bearish on a particular stock or market. This strategy involves buying a put option at a higher strike price and selling a put option at a lower strike price. The goal is to profit from a decline in the stock price while limiting potential losses.

The Bear Put Spread is a popular strategy because it provides a limited risk profile and has a defined maximum profit potential. It can be used to profit from a moderate decline in the stock price or to protect against a more significant downturn.

Calendar Spread

The Calendar Spread strategy discussed above can also be used in a bearish market. By selling a near-term call option and buying a longer-term call option with the same strike price, traders can profit from the difference in time decay between the two options.

In a bearish market, traders can use the Calendar Spread strategy to profit from the expected decline in the stock price. They can also adjust the strategy by buying a put option instead of a call option, depending on their outlook.

Iron Condor

The Iron Condor can be used in a bearish market. This strategy involves selling both a call option and a put option with higher strike prices, and buying both a call option and a put option with lower strike prices.

The goal of the Iron Condor strategy is to profit from a narrow range of price movements in the stock or market while limiting potential losses. It can be a useful strategy in a bearish market because it allows traders to profit from a small decline in the stock price while limiting potential losses in the event of a more significant downturn.

For example, if a stock is trading at $100, you expect minimal movement over a specified period of time. Basically, a trader enters a bear call credit spread—say, selling the $105 call and buying the $110 call—for a net credit of $100.

Then the trader enters a bull put spread, selling the $95 put and buying the $90 put for another $1.00 credit.

If the price stays within the width of the $10 spread, the maximum profit is $2.00. The maximum loss (assuming only one $5.00 side is breached, is $3.00 ($5 width minus the $2.00 credit).

Simple Hedging Strategies

Protective Collar

A Protective Collar is a popular hedging strategy used by investors who are looking to protect their stock portfolio against potential losses. This strategy involves purchasing a put option to protect against downside risk and simultaneously selling a call option to generate income and offset the cost of the put option.

The Protective Collar strategy is a useful tool for managing risk because it provides a degree of downside protection while still allowing investors to participate in the potential upside of their stock portfolio. It is a flexible strategy that can be adjusted to suit different market conditions.

Married Put

The Married Put is another hedging strategy that can be used by investors to protect their stock portfolio against potential losses. This strategy involves purchasing a put option for each share of stock held in the portfolio. The put option provides protection against downside risk while the stock itself can still appreciate in value. Fundamentally, the married put is the Protective Collar without selling a call to help pay for the insurance.

The Married Put strategy is particularly useful for investors who are bullish on a particular stock or market but want to protect against potential losses. It allows investors to participate in the potential upside of their stock portfolio while still limiting potential losses in the event of a downturn.

Collar vs. Married Put

While both the Protective Collar and Married Put strategies can be used to hedge against potential losses, they differ in their approaches. The Protective Collar involves selling a call option to offset the cost of a put option, while the Married Put involves purchasing a put option for each share of stock held in the portfolio.

The Protective Collar is a more complex strategy that requires careful management, while the Married Put is a simpler approach that provides more straightforward protection against downside risk. Ultimately, the choice between the two strategies will depend on the investor's goals, risk tolerance, and market outlook.

Choosing the Right Hedging Strategy

When it comes to hedging strategies, there is no one-size-fits-all approach. The right strategy will depend on a variety of factors, including the investor's goals, risk tolerance, and market outlook.

Overall, the key to successful hedging is to strike a balance between protecting against potential losses and participating in the potential upside of your portfolio.

14

UNDERSTANDING OPTION GREEKS MINI PRIMER

Option Greeks are a series of mathematical measurements that are used to quantify different aspects of options trading. These measurements can be used to better understand and analyze the risks and potential rewards of different trading strategies and can help traders make more informed decisions about their investments.

There are five primary option Greeks that traders need to be familiar with: Delta, Gamma, Theta, Vega, and Rho. Each of these Greeks measures a different aspect of options trading, and understanding how they work can be crucial to success in the market. I have discussed them below (Charles Schwab, 2021):

Delta

Delta is perhaps the most well-known of the Option Greeks. It measures the rate of change in an option's price in relation to changes in the price of the underlying asset. In other words, Delta measures how much an option's price is likely to move in response to a change in the price of the underlying stock. Delta can range from 0 to 1 for call options and from 0 to -1 for put options.

For example, a call option with a delta of 0.5 means that the option's price will increase by $0.50 for every $1 increase in the underlying asset's price. Furthermore, a Delta of 0.5 can be interpreted as a 50% chance that the option will expire in the money.

It's important to note that Delta is not a fixed value and can change as the underlying asset's price and time until expiration change. As an option gets closer to expiration, the Delta of the option can increase or decrease rapidly, indicating a higher or lower probability of the option expiring in the money.

Delta is a handy tool for traders to assess their risk exposure when trading options. It enables traders to determine whether they have a long or short-directional bias on the underlying asset by examining the Delta of their portfolio. If a trader has a net long Delta, they are essentially optimistic about the underlying asset and would profit from a price rise. In this case, Delta's would be positive. In contrast, if a trader has a net short Delta, they are essentially bearish on the underlying asset and would profit from a price decline. Delta can be a valuable indicator for traders to keep an eye on their portfolio's risk and make necessary adjustments to their positions.

Gamma

Gamma is a measure of the rate of change in Delta itself. This means that Gamma can help traders predict how much an option's Delta is likely to change in response to changes in the underlying asset's price. This information can be crucial when trying to fine-tune an options trading strategy.

Gamma can range from 0 to positive infinity for both calls and put options. Gamma is highest for at-the-money options and decreases as options move further in or out-of-the-money. If a trader has a portfolio with a high Gamma, it means that the portfolio's Delta will change quickly with even small movements in the underlying stock's price.

This can be both a good and a bad thing. On the one hand, a high Gamma can allow a trader to quickly adjust their portfolio to changes in the market, enabling them to capture profits when the market moves in their favor. On the other hand, a high Gamma can also lead to large losses if the market moves against the trader.

Theta

Theta is a favorite time-machine tool for Weekly option sellers to gauge the rate at which an option's value is likely to decline over time.

As an option nears its expiration date, its Theta value will increase, reflecting the fact that the option is losing value with each passing day. Theta is always negative for options because the value of an option decreases as time passes.

Theta is an options seller's best friend!

Traders who use options as a short-term trading strategy, such as weekly options, must pay particular attention to Theta. As the expiration date approaches, an option's Theta value increases, which means that the option loses value at a faster rate. This is because the likelihood of the option expiring in the money decreases over time, and this decreased probability reduces the option's overall value. Theta is highest for at-the-money options, and it is essential to monitor this value closely as it can significantly impact the profitability of an option position.

Vega

Vega is a measure of how much an option's price is affected by changes in the volatility of the underlying asset. When the volatility of the underlying asset increases, Vega also increases, as options become more valuable in volatile markets.

Vega can be positive or negative and is highest for at-the-money options. Higher volatility often results in higher option prices, while lower volatility results in lower option prices. For traders who sell weekly options for premium, understanding Vega is crucial because they are taking on the risk of market volatility.

As a result, any increase or decrease in volatility can significantly affect the option's price, and traders must estimate this impact to manage their risk properly. Calculating the potential impact of Vega on a weekly option is a valuable way for traders to manage their risk effectively.

Trading platforms often provide a Vega calculation, which estimates how much an option's price may change for every 1% increase or decrease in implied volatility. For instance, if a trader sells a weekly put option on a stock with a Vega of 0.05 and the implied volatility of the underlying stock increases by 1%, they can expect the price of the option to go up by roughly 0.05.

Conversely, if the implied volatility of the underlying stock decreases by 1%, they can expect the price of the option to decrease by approximately 0.05. Understanding this information helps traders adjust their positions accordingly and manage their risk effectively.

Rho

Rho is the Greek that measures how an option's price changes in response to shifts in interest rates. Of all the Greeks, Rho is the least important for traders. It is included here for awareness. Rho is positive for call options and negative for put options. When interest rates go up, call option prices increase, and put option prices decrease, and vice versa when interest rates decrease.

When traders sell options, they are essentially loaning money to the buyer of the option and receiving interest in the form of premium payments. As interest rates fluctuate, the value of this interest can also shift, which can have a significant impact on the profitability of the trade.

Let's say a trader decides to sell a weekly call option for a $1 premium on a stock trading at $55, with a strike price of $50 and a Rho of 0.05, assuming a risk-free interest rate of 2%. This means that if the interest rate increases by 1%, the option's price may increase by $0.05, which would reduce the profitability of the trade.

For instance, if the interest rate rises to 3%, the option's price may increase to $1.05. Conversely, if the interest rate decreases, the option premium may also decrease, making the trade more profitable. If the risk-free interest rate drops to 1%, the option's price may decrease to $0.95, increasing the profitability of the trade.

Option Greeks are critical to options trading, and understanding the primary Greeks is crucial for success in the market.

15

THE KACHING METHOD FOR SMALL ACCOUNTS

When it comes to trading options on smaller accounts, say $10,000 and under, traders need to be precise in their methods.

Also, accounts under $25,000 need to be aware of what the Securities and Exchange Commission (SEC) defines as a Pattern Day Trader. Under this rule, if you make 4 or more round trip trades in 5 business days that represent more than 6% of your total trades, you will be classified as a Pattern Day Trader and will be restricted to opening more trades.

Always check with your brokerage account for precise definitions and how they may apply to your account.

For KaChing traders using weekly options, this is generally fine because you can put on 3 KaChings per week and be safe. Your long puts will go out the same 90 or 120 days and you will be rolling over the three positions. We will get into specifics a little further on.

SOME DO'S AND DON'TS

Focus on Liquidity:

Stick to trading options on stocks that have high liquidity.

Liquidity refers to the ease with which a trader can enter and exit positions in the market without significantly impacting the price. It is essential to focus on trading options on stocks or indices that have high liquidity (trading volume).

One of the primary benefits of trading weekly options on heavily traded underlying assets is the tighter bid-ask spreads. The bid-ask spread represents the difference between the price a buyer is willing to pay (bid) and the price a seller is asking (ask).

In liquid markets, the bid-ask spreads tend to be narrower, meaning that the difference between the buying and selling price is relatively smaller.

A narrower bid-ask spread is advantageous for traders with small trading accounts because it can help minimize transaction costs. When the spread is tight, traders can enter and exit positions more efficiently, resulting in lower slippage and reduced trading expenses.

Let's consider an example to illustrate the impact of liquidity on trading costs. Suppose you are interested in trading weekly call options on a heavily traded stock with high liquidity. The bid price for the call option is $2.50, and the ask price is $2.55. In this case, the bid-ask spread is only $0.05, indicating a tight spread. If you decide to buy the option at the ask price and later sell it at the bid price, the spread of $0.05 represents your transaction cost for the trade.

Now, let's compare this to a scenario where you attempt to trade a weekly call option on a less liquid stock. The bid price for the call option is $2.45, and the ask price is $2.70. Here, the wider bid-ask spread of $0.25 increases your transaction costs. If you buy at the ask price and sell at the bid price, the spread of $0.25 becomes your cost, significantly higher than in the previous example.

Trading options on liquid stocks or indices not only minimizes transaction costs but also improves trade execution. In liquid markets, there is a greater number of buyers and sellers actively participating, creating a more competitive environment.

As a result, orders are executed more quickly and at prices closer to the desired levels, reducing the potential for slippage.

Additionally, liquidity plays a crucial role in managing risk. When options are illiquid, it can be challenging to close out a position or adjust strategies quickly. This lack of liquidity can leave traders vulnerable to unexpected market movements, limiting their ability to protect profits or cut losses efficiently. In contrast, liquid markets offer greater flexibility, enabling traders to react promptly to changing market conditions.

To identify options with high liquidity, it is advisable to look for stocks or indices that are actively traded, have a large market capitalization, and significant trading volumes. Popular stocks from well-established companies and broad-based indices tend to meet these criteria.

Traders can also refer to metrics like average daily trading volume and open interest to assess the liquidity of specific options contracts.

Start Small:

When it comes to trading with a small trading account, it is crucial to manage risk effectively. One of the best practices for traders with limited capital is to start small and gradually increase position sizes as they gain experience and confidence.

For example, let's say a trader has a small trading account of $5,000. Instead of diving in and risking a large portion of their capital on a single trade, they decide to start with only 1 or 2 contracts. By doing so, they can control the amount of capital at risk and prevent a substantial loss from wiping out their account.

Starting small also allows traders to assess the effectiveness of their strategies without incurring excessive losses. It provides an opportunity to identify strengths and weaknesses in their approach and make necessary adjustments. Traders can analyze their trades, review their risk-reward ratios, and fine-tune their strategies based on real-world outcomes.

As traders gain experience and confidence, they can gradually increase their position sizes while continuing to manage risk effectively. This gradual approach enables them to grow their trading account over time without exposing themselves to unnecessary risks.

Another benefit of starting small is that it helps traders overcome emotional biases that can negatively impact decision-making. When trading with a small account, the fear of losing a significant portion of capital is reduced. This allows traders to focus on following their trading plan and making rational decisions based on market analysis rather than succumbing to emotional impulses.

Define Your Risk Parameters:

Determine your risk tolerance and set clear guidelines for position sizing and stop-loss levels. Weekly options can be volatile, so establishing a predetermined risk threshold for each trade helps maintain discipline and prevents excessive losses.

One of the first steps in defining risk parameters is determining your risk tolerance. Every trader has a different comfort level when it comes to risk. Some traders may be more conservative, preferring to minimize risk and protect capital, while others may be willing to take on more risk for potentially higher returns. Understanding your risk tolerance helps you establish appropriate risk management strategies that align with your personal preferences.

Once you have identified your risk tolerance, it is crucial to set clear guidelines for position sizing. Position sizing refers to determining the number of contracts or the amount of capital you are willing to allocate to each trade. It is an essential component of risk management as it helps control the potential impact of losses on your trading account.

For example, in the KaChing Method Trading Plan, we outlined risk parameters for a $50,000 account where we allocated $10,000 in capital to be deployed weekly. In this case we had each trade at a maximum of 3% of the $50,000 or total risk at $1500 per trade.

If you have a $10,000 account – the $1500 risk per trade in my opinion is valid, however this is now 15% of the total account. There is no getting around that. You could do 1 contract and have total risk at $500, which is 5% - however you are still limited to under 4 trades per week – let's just say you are taking 3 KaChings a week.

Another factor is looking at the option chains for your trade candidates and checking what increments the strike prices are set. Some stocks have $5 increments, meaning if you sell a $100 put for the weekly, the long is minimally $95. That may be too broad. It is best to find highly liquid stocks that have $1.00 increments so you can have much tighter spreads and therefore less risk.

Use Options Strategies Wisely:

Explore strategies that align with your risk profile and trading goals. For example, vertical spreads, such as credit spreads can be suitable for limited-risk strategies. These strategies allow you to control risk while still benefiting from the shorter time frame of weekly options.

KaChing Trades are credit spreads, a type of vertical spread where you receive net credit when establishing the trade.

Credit spreads as we outlined provide an opportunity to generate income while still benefiting from the shorter time frame of weekly options. Since you receive a credit when establishing the trade, your risk is limited to the difference between the strike prices of the options minus the net credit received.

Vertical spreads in general are options strategies that simultaneously involve buying and selling options of the same type (either calls or puts) but with different strike prices. The goal of a vertical spread is to capitalize on the price movement of the underlying asset while controlling risk.

Debit spreads can be another suitable option strategy for limited-risk approaches when trading weekly options. While you pay a debit to establish the trade, the risk is predefined and limited to the net debit paid.

For instance, let's say a trader has a bullish outlook on a stock trading at $70 and decides to trade a bullish debit spread using weekly call options. The trader buys a call option with a strike price of $65 for a premium of $2.00 and simultaneously sells a call option with a strike price of $70 for a premium of $1.00. The net debit paid is $1.00 ($2.00 - $1.00). The maximum potential loss for this debit spread would be $1.00, which is the net debit paid.

These types of trades can be used to supersize KaChing Trades as outlined in Chapter 13. In a very favorable market, we typically put on these trades using monthly options for extra income. For small accounts, this is important because it does not break the 4 trades per week Pattern Day Trader rule.

We will go into a lot more specific detail for lots of trade examples in the full book, coming soon!

Stick to Your Trading Plan:

Go back to Chapter 11, What is a Trading Plan and How to Create One and if you have a smaller account, make the modifications. The beauty of the plan is that the only things that change are a modification of the numbers and reanalyzing your risk tolerances. If three $5 spread contracts with a total risk of $1500, or 15% is too much, then scale it back. Start at 1 contract and build up.

Once you get going and are comfortable, things will be easy to scale.

Diversify Your Trades:

For any account this is key, for small accounts it is very critical. If you have three bank trades or 3 energy trades and anything happens in those sectors, you are at risk and rolling forward.

It is better to have 3-5 sectors on your radar that are performing and have a trade those as a basket. You can keep track of the hot sectors in many online sites, Investor's Business Daily does a great job.

It's important to note that diversification does not guarantee profits or eliminate all risks, but it can help manage risk exposure and improve the overall risk-reward profile of your trading strategy.

Summary:

Traders with small accounts can use weekly options in a variety of ways and grow their account significantly – a lot higher than our .5% to 1% per week. In fact, using vertical spreads as outlined may yield 10-15% per month if trades are profitable.

16

RESOURCES

Here some handy resources.

KaChing Tracker Blank

Here is the tracker that you can copy or scan and keep manually. If you want the Excel Tracker, email us at info@kachingweeklyoptions.com

Note:

We have no affiliate arrangement or profit in any way from these recommendations.

Investor's Business Daily – To me the holy grail for insights, accumulation / distribution ratings, sector heat maps – everything.

https://www.investors.com/

The Motley Fool – Great market insights, stock picks, portfolios and more.

https://www.fool.com/

Seeking Alpha – Stock market educations, picks, great analysis.

https://seekingalpha.com/

Mind Valley – Wonder education and learning community for a better you. Amazing self help courses, manifesting all your desires, how to overcome just about all challenges.

https://www.mindvalley.com/

CONCLUSION

The first step to becoming an options trader is to understand the concept itself and all the terminologies that go along with it. Options are contracts that give the holder the right but not the obligation to trade the underlying. You can either be an options buyer or a seller; the buyer holds the options contract while the seller *writes* the contracts. There are two types of options traded on the market: call options and put options. Both types of options give the option buyer the right but not the obligation to trade the underlying stock at a fixed price called the strike price. The difference between the strike price and the market price of the underlying is referred to as the option's internal value. It is also the potential profit a buyer will make should they exercise their right. The option seller, on the other hand, is only entitled to the price paid for the options, i.e., the premiums. The buyer can exercise their right at any time as long as the option contract hasn't expired.

The major reasons we trade weekly options are the following:

- Weekly options are cheaper to trade due to low premium prices and a faster rate of time decay.
- We can trade four times more than we can with standard options and also have the potential to yield better profits in a shorter time.
- The waiting time for options to expire and trade closed is cut tremendously with weekly options.
- Large-volume stocks offer weekly options, making market opportunities readily available.

Why wait 30 days when we can make money consistently every week by using the cream tub KaChing formula? We buy one long-dated put—this is our insurance—and sort of sell back the long-dated put in smaller chunks at a profit. I trade it in four simple steps, knowing that Delta will always be our friend:

1. Choose a stock and understand its behavior
2. Buy a long-dated put with a life span of 120 days as insurance

3. Sell a short-dated put with a life span of 1 week and receive immediate cash

4. Manage, rinse, and repeat.

The above is just a summarized example of a trading plan that erases the interference of emotions from our trades and ensures we stay within a predefined risk range and goals.

Emotion, the culprit responsible for the losses incurred by retail traders, can be controlled, but you'd need to put in some work. First, you must build confidence and become conversant with the trade like you would in any other profession. Never stop learning new ways to exploit the market and developing plans that'll put you one step ahead of your opposition. Be sincere with yourself and study what worked and what didn't; to do this, you'd have to keep a journal of all your trades, recording every detail about every trade. Make necessary changes, dissolve non-profitable strategies, and make new ones.

Never for once think trading is for men in suits. NO! Anyone with the right mindset can become a successful trader. I can say that because I've been there myself. Things turned out great for me when I realized that "the goal of a successful trader is to make the best trades. Money is secondary" (AZQuotes, n.d.).

By the time you get here, I'm confident that you're not the same trader who allowed their emotions to be carried by the wind. Reading this book tells me you're putting in the work, and I would love to get some feedback on the level of impact this book has had on your trading journey. May the market trends be with us!